Cultural Sovereignty

Isaiah Litvak
Christopher Maule

The Praeger Special Studies program—utilizing the most modern and efficient book production techniques and a selective worldwide distribution network—makes available to the academic, government, and business communities significant, timely research in U.S. and international economic, social, and political development.

Cultural Sovereignty
The Time and Reader's Digest Case in Canada

PRAEGER SPECIAL STUDIES IN INTERNATIONAL POLITICS AND GOVERNMENT

Praeger Publishers   New York   Washington   London

Library of Congress Cataloging in Publication Data

Litvak, Isaiah A
    Cultural sovereignty.

    (Praeger special studies in international
politics and government)
    1. Canadian periodicals. 2. American
periodicals—Canada. 3. Canada—Relations
(General) with the United States. 4. United
States—Relations (General) with Canada.
I. Maule, Christopher J., 1934-   joint author.
II. Title.
PN4914.P4L5   051   73-13342

PRAEGER PUBLISHERS
111 Fourth Avenue, New York, N.Y. 10003, U.S.A.
5, Cromwell Place, London SW7 2JL, England

Published in the United States of America in 1974
by Praeger Publishers, Inc.

Printed in the United States of America

ACKNOWLEDGMENTS

A number of people assisted us in the preparation of this study. We want to express a special debt of gratitude to our research assistant, Paul Hanrahan, for the dedication with which he worked on the original manuscript, and we are also grateful for the editorial assistance we received from Professor David Farr and Alexander Ross. The material in the study was prepared readily and efficiently because of the help of our secretary, Joan Hamilton, to whom we are indebted. None of these individuals, however, is responsible for the contents of the study. The authors gratefully acknowledge the financial assistance provided by the Canada Council.

CONTENTS

LISTS OF TABLES AND FIGURES

Cultural Sovereignty

In the 1970s Canadian nationalism will continue to
center largely on the issue of control--specifically, the
loss of Canadian control to U.S. interests. Since Confederation, Canadians have expressed the fear of being canni-
balized by the United States; this concern has been expressed
in many economic, political, and sociocultural issues and
has continued over the years because of the apparent ease
with which the United States has been able to establish
economic influence in Canada; in fact, some Canadians perceive the United States as the metropolitan power in relation to Canada, which they view as a hinterland region.

Since the mid-1950s Canadians have been subjected to
a barrage of official reports, academic studies, and newspaper and magazine articles, in company with verbalized
prejudices, concerning the effects of direct foreign investment in Canada. The more detailed studies have tried to
come to grips with the economic effects of direct foreign
investment, while giving token recognition to the political
and sociocultural effects as well. It has been much more
difficult to identify, and especially to quantify, the political and sociocultural effects at all, and thus these
are areas where emotion and prejudice can be and have been
freely expressed.

Foreign Direct Investment in Canada, the most recent
government-commissioned study on foreign ownership in Canada, devotes only eight pages to its examination of the impact of foreign control of Canadian business on Canadian
culture and society.[1] Before proceeding to comment on some
of its findings, note should be taken of the study's definition of the term "culture":

> Culture is not simply the arts, architecture,
> films, books, sculpture and paintings of a na-
> tion. Culture is the historically developed
> values and patterns of behavior covering the
> whole range of human activity. Quite simply,
> the culture of a people is its entire way of
> life.[2]

The government's study acknowledges that because
Canada is an open society and lacks a strong national identity it is more susceptible to foreign influence, thus further inhibiting the ability of Canadians to develop their
own distinctive national identity. This problem is aggravated by the fact that many of the critical industries that
involve themselves in the dissemination of culture, such as
book publishing and film and book distribution, are U.S.-
controlled. Moreover, many of the Canadian-owned firms in
these and other industries seem to exist to Americanize
Canadian tastes for U.S.-designed products manufactured by
U.S. subsidiaries in Canada.

Canadian broadcasting policy is at present one of the
few Canadian policies that includes foreign ownership restrictions designed to protect and promote Canadian culture.
Section 3(b) of the Broadcasting Act reads as follows:
"The Canadian broadcasting system should be effectively
owned and controlled by Canadians so as to safeguard, en-
rich and strengthen the cultural, political, social and
economic fabric of Canada."[3] This act encompasses conven-
tional broadcasting as well as cable television under the
Canadian Radio-Television Commission (C.R.T.C.), which
stipulates that

> broadcasting licences may not be issued and re-
> newals of broadcasting licences may not be granted
> to applicants . . . who are not Canadian citizens
> or eligible Canadian corporations; . . . [or to]
> governments of countries other than Canada or of
> political subdivisions of countries other than
> Canada and agents of such governments.[4]

In order to ensure that the ownership regulations are
not undermined by the program content of Canadian broadcasting firms, which may transmit mainly U.S. programs, the
C.R.T.C. has strengthened its regulations concerning Canadian program content to make the social, political, and cultural objectives of the Broadcasting Act impossible to
thwart. Although Canadian broadcasting policy emphasizes

the nourishing of Canadian culture, which often requires
protection in the face of foreign investment and competition,
it does not specify what should be protected nor predict
what would happen in the absence of protection.

To illustrate some of the political and cultural implications of direct foreign investment in Canada we have
chosen to examine, by way of a case study, the Canadian
periodical industry, which suits our purposes in a number
of ways. It has recognized cultural attributes; its economic aspects can be studied; it consists of both Canadian-
owned and foreign-owned firms; and these firms have presented written briefs to the hearings of the Royal Commission on Publications[5] and the Senate Committee on the Mass
Media.[6] Further, two of the leading firms in this industry
are U.S.-controlled--Time and Reader's Digest. Although
these two publications have been the focus of many contro-
versies, they have managed to escape the impact of every
key proposal that would either have identified them as non-
Canadian periodicals or have limited the competitive advantages arising from their economic ties to U.S. parent firms.
We shall examine some of the political ramifications of foreign investment in this industry by studying and comparing
the presentations and policy recommendations made by the
domestic and foreign firms and by following through to see
whose views prevailed and, hopefully, why they prevailed.

The purpose of this study is to examine the role and
posture of domestic and foreign periodical publishers in
Canada, as evidenced by their presentations to the Royal
Commission on Publications and the Senate Committee on the
Mass Media and their reactions to recommendations made and
policies proposed and implemented. In addition we hope to
discover whether the attitudes of Canadian-owned periodicals
reflect a desire for commercial protection or a desire to
protect Canada's cultural identity. This discussion will
provide a way of introducing the policy alternatives that
exist for the Canadian government in the 1970s.

We will examine the evolution of the consumer periodical industry* in Canada from 1867 to 1971, describing the
firms involved and their attitudes and economic importance,

_____

*The Royal Commission distinguished between "consumer"
and "business" periodicals on the basis of whether they
provided entertainment and general information (consumer),
or commercial or vocational information (business). The
commission studied scholarly and cultural journals as well
as consumer and business periodicals.

the cultural issues, the public policies suggested and implemented, and the reaction to these policies that took
place within the industry. Detailed attention will be
given to the period from 1960 to the present, with chapters
devoted to the Royal Commission on Publications and the
Senate Committee on the Mass Media. At each stage we will
undertake an analysis of the attitudes and influence of
domestic and foreign periodical publishers and their concern with protectionism and Canadian culture.

In the chapters that follow we will deal with the historical background (1867-1960) of the periodical industry,
with the hearings before the Royal Commission on Publications, with the report of the Royal Commission and the industry's reaction to it, and with the Senate Committee on
the Mass Media; and, finally, we will make some concluding
observations and suggested policy alternatives. However,
before proceeding, we will outline the sociocultural role
of periodicals and publishing as we have perceived it to be.

SOCIOCULTURAL ROLE OF PERIODICALS

Each society has its own value system. However, the
increasing interaction between the organizations and per-
sons of different societies now makes it virtually impossible for any nation state to prevent foreign influences
from affecting its value system. Social interactions take
place in the economic, sociocultural, and political spheres
and include the movement of goods, capital, technology,
and people. Even in our world of increasing interdependen-
cies, however, most societies try to protect and enhance
those of their institutions that promote social cohesion.
These institutions invariably include the various forms of
mass media, which interpret and communicate events and issues, both at home and abroad, in the context of the historical experience and traditional values of each society.

For this reason many Canadians express a growing concern about the powerful presence of foreign influence, specifically that of the United States over Canadian mass
media, which may have the effect of Americanizing the value
structure of Canadian society; this would make it difficult
for Canadians to promote a value system reflective of
"things Canadian," rather than of "things U.S." Preoccupation with the racial problems in the United States, with
the Vietnam war, and with U.S. elections, as transmitted
through U.S. television, radio, and byproduct and spillover
circulation of U.S. magazines, have so sensitized most Ca-

nadians that certain important issues and events in Canada
seem to occupy a secondary place of importance in their
day-to-day concern. French Canadians are the key exception
to this observation. The present cultural and political
debate in Quebec, and its language barrier, mitigate the
impact of the U.S. mass media, and, thus, the degree of
exposure to U.S. attitudes. Kenneth Boulding has noted
the importance to a society of having an image of itself:

> In tracing the effect of images on the course of
> history, peculiar attention must be paid to the
> images of time and especially the images of the
> future. Curiously enough, it may not be so much
> the actual content of the image of the future
> which is important in its effect, but its general
> quality of optimism or pessimism, certainty or
> uncertainty, breadth or narrowness. . . . The in-
> dividual or the nation which has no sense of di-
> rection in time, no sense of clear future ahead,
> is likely to be vacillating, uncertain in be-
> haviour, and to have a poor chance of surviving.[7]

Few intelligent people would argue that a nation can
or should isolate itself from the reach of foreign mass
media, electronically or otherwise. But one cannot ignore
the fact that the mass media are an ideological instrument
and that the ownership of this instrument constitutes a
part of the power base of a society.[8] To allow control of
any part of the mass media to fall into foreign hands would
have important social and political implications.

The news media have long been recognized as having an
important influence on people's views and opinions of
events. For example, the close control of the editorial
content of Reader's Digest Canada by the U.S. parent company, and the requirement that most articles be written
for the U.S. edition, not only limit the effectiveness of
the Canadian contribution but also provide a U.S. slant to
the range of selection available.[9] Throughout the 1950s,
Reader's Digest encouraged the publication and dissemination of politically oriented articles in support of the
Taiwan regime, while maintaining a highly critical view of
"Mainland" China--a view that on occasion was even more
critical than that of the U.S. government; a similar posture
has been evident toward Cuba. Yet throughout this period
the Canadian government and certain Canadians in responsible positions were attempting to promote Canadian relations
with both of these countries, and with the exception of a

very few inconsequential Canadian magazines, Canadian periodicals were largely in support of the Canadian government position regardless of their political leanings.

The question to raise is not whether Canadians should be denied the opportunity of reading foreign publications, but whether a foreign publication, the editorial policy of which is formulated in another country in the context of its value system, should be allowed to print under a Canadian guise and be assisted in this pretense by Canadian legislation. An equally important question to raise is whether the continued presence of the Canadian editions of Reader's Digest and Time undermines the promotion and enhancement of "Canadian" magazines that might otherwise become national in scope and content.

Other Canadian studies have been made on this question. The Royal Commission on Publications gave detailed consideration to the role of periodicals as a medium for criticism, informed debate and discussion, and the search for truth, with democratic government viewed as being government by communication.[10] The role of periodicals as part of the communications media was emphasized as follows:

> In this role, communications are the thread which
> binds together the fibers of a nation. They can
> protect a nation's values and encourage their
> practice. They can make democratic government
> possible and better government probable. They
> can soften sectional asperities and bring honorable compromises. They can inform and educate
> in the arts, the sciences and commerce. They
> can help market a nation's products and promote
> its material wealth. In these functions it may
> be claimed--claimed without much challenge--that
> the communications of a nation are as vital to its
> life as its defences, and should receive at least
> as great a measure of national protection.[11]

The commission expressed concern lest there be a reduction in the number of distinct Canadian voices through increased concentration of the ownership of Canadian periodicals and, more importantly, through the elimination of Canadian periodicals because of increased distribution of periodicals from the United States. However, the commission was quite clear in its recognition of the cultural relationship of Canada with the United States:

> The Commission has rejected, too, the too-widely
> voiced opinion that the culture of the American

people is in some way an alien culture, a mono-
lithic, inferior way of life from which Canadians
need shelter. The Commission has preferred to
believe that the people of Canada, like the people of the United States, are basically North
Americans, inheritors of the thought and traditions of Europe, but also the children of geography, products of the environments, the emotions,
the driving forces, the faith, the dreams and
the forms of expression of the North American
continent.[12]

Although acknowledging the similarities of the two cultures, the commission emphasized that the political, social,
and economic tasks and problems of the two countries do
differ, as do the environments in which they are experienced.
Therefore it was stated that Canadian tasks and problems

cannot be approached understandingly or usefully
by communications media owned or controlled in
another country, even though that country be
friendly. Only a truly Canadian printing press,
one with the "feel" of Canada and directly responsible to Canada, can give us the critical
analysis, the informed discourse and dialogue
which are indispensable in a sovereign society.[13]

It was also stressed that non-Canadians should be able to
read about Canada through "Canadian eyes."[14]
Apart from emphasizing the importance of these social
values, the commission also recognized a government responsibility to promote Canadian publishers, writers, painters,
and photographers, and pointed out that failure to support
Canadian periodical writers would soon lead to problems
for authors of books and the book publishing industry,[15] a
theme that has since been taken up by national media.
The importance of magazines as a special part of the
communications media was stressed in the report of the
Senate Committee:

Magazines are special. Magazines constitute the
only national press we possess in Canada. Magazines add a journalistic dimension which no other
medium can provide--depth and wholeness and tex-
ture, plus the visual impact of graphic design.
Magazines, because of their freedom from daily
deadlines, can aspire to a level of excellence

that is seldom attainable in other media. Magazines, in a different way from any other medium,
can help foster in Canadians a sense of themselves. In terms of cultural survival, magazines
could potentially be as important as railroads,
airlines, national broadcasting networks, and
national hockey leagues.[16]

In addition to the foregoing, Canadian views on the
sociocultural role of the communications media, of which
periodicals are a part, can be found in reports dealing
with radio and television broadcasting and book publishing.
It is interesting to note the repeated emphasis the following reports give to the cultural contribution of the media
and to the threat to Canadian culture that is perceived to
come from the United States. The "overflow" of the media
into Canada from the south was found to exist in radio,
television, and book publishing as well as in periodicals.
The 1929 Report of the Royal Commission on Radio Broadcasting viewed the communications media, especially broadcasting, as an instrument for the education of Canadians
and expressed concern that, because of the number of programs originating outside of Canada, there would be

a tendency to mould the minds of the young people
in the homes to ideals and opinions that are not
Canadian. In a country of the vast geographical
dimensions of Canada, broadcasting will undoubtedly become a great force in fostering a national
spirit and interpreting national citizenship.[17]

The Report of the Royal Commission on National Development in the Arts, Letters and Sciences followed up on some
of the points raised by the 1929 report on broadcasting.
In particular it stressed the contribution of a nationally
controlled system of broadcasting to Canadian unity and to
the development of "a truly Canadian cultural life."[18]
Newspapers and periodicals were singled out as the best
ways to supply people with the information they needed, to
make the judgments necessary for the sound functioning of
a democratic society. "The newspaper and periodical press
of Canada . . . provides most of the reading matter of most
Canadians, and . . . is still probably the chief source of
knowledge to Canadians of their country and of one another."[19]
The commission's discussion of the media was set within a
framework of warning about the impact of American influences
on Canadian life.

It cannot be denied, however, that a vast and disproportionate amount of material coming from a
single alien source may stifle rather than stimu-
late our own creative effort; and, passively accepted without any standard of comparison, this
may weaken critical faculties. We are now spend-
ing millions to maintain a national independence
which would be nothing but an empty shell without
a vigorous and distinctive cultural life. We have
seen that we have its elements in our traditions
and in our history; we have made important progress, often aided by American generosity. We
must not be blind, however, to the very present
danger of permanent dependence.[20]

It was noted that

many Canadians in the 1920's . . . began to fear
that cultural annexation would follow our absorption into the American radio system just as surely
as economic and even political annexation would
have followed absorption into the American railway system fifty years earlier. Thoughtful people
were deeply perturbed and some were aware even of
a new national crisis.[21]

Similar comments about the cultural influence of the
American media appeared in two later reports. In the first,
reference was made to the economies of scale in communication, which tend to undermine the development of separate
Canadian media.

It is equally clear that we could have cheaper
radio and television service if Canadian stations
became outlets of American networks. However,
if the less costly method is always chosen, is
it possible to have a Canadian nation at all?
The Canadian answer, irrespective of party or
race, has been uniformly the same for nearly a
century. We are prepared, by measures of assistance, financial aid and conscious stimulation,
to compensate for our disabilities of geography,
sparse population and vast distances, and we have
accepted this as a legitimate role of government
in Canada.[22]

In the second an attempt was made to distinguish between
nationalism and protectionism for certain groups in Canada.

The requirement that the broadcasting service
should be basically Canadian in content and
character is not an attempt to exploit nationalism for the benefit of Canadian artists,
writers, performers and producers. Its purpose
is to recognize that Canadians have ideas to
express and should have access to communications
media linked so closely to public property.[23]

In the White Paper on Broadcasting in 1966 it was reiterated that a distinctly Canadian broadcasting system was
necessary in order to assure a Canadian national identity
and Canadian unity;[24] the Broadcasting Act of 1968 put
these views into legislation.[25]

The Canadian Radio-Television Commission (C.R.T.C.)
provides further insight into the perceived sociocultural
role of broadcasting. Linking broadcasting to the other
media, the C.R.T.C. notes,

The Royal Commission on Publications (1960-61)
had said that "the communications of a nation
are as vital to its life as its defenses." It
has been the Commission's view, that Canada must
at this time inject an extra measure of effort
into the development of the Canadian Broadcasting
System.[26]

But like the "defenses" of a nation, broadcasting
must serve yet other objectives to "safeguard, en-
rich and strengthen . . . the fabric." This calls
for "Canadian" content, forms and functions in
broadcast programming.[27]

Later reports of the C.R.T.C. stress the way in which
a national communications system must be responsible for
"identifying and strengthening cultural entities, regional
identities and community loyalties."[28]

Pierre Juneau, chairman of the C.R.T.C., describes the
homogenizing force of the media in North America, the need
to provide diversity for Canadians, and the economies of
scale that affect the media:

The task which confronts us is to find ways of adding to the choice that is offered to Canadians not
of reducing it. The Commission is arguing that
unless we do something about it, Canadians are going to have their choices dictated to them by a

distribution system which will inevitably find
it more economic to pipe all over Canada the
overflow of mass produced American programs rather
than to support the production of programs that
are relevant to Canadians. The Commission is also
arguing that such a dumping system will gradually
weaken Canadian stations and deprive them of the
capacity to improve or even to maintain adequate
Canadian service.[29]

This sociocultural importance to Canada has been as-
cribed to book publishing as well as to broadcasting, both
by the Ontario and federal governments. The Ontario Government Royal Commission on Book Publishing reported that

Canadian book publishing is an industry which is
of major importance in creating that sense of
identity, political, historical, and cultural,
which is Canadianism. Moreover, English-language
book publishing in this country is predominantly
an Ontario industry, and this province therefore
has a special responsibility to nurture and encourage it.[30]

Gérard Pelletier, when Secretary of State, wrote that
a country cannot abandon its cultural resources to foreigners for fear of absorption, and that "a Canadian publishing
industry inspired, financed and controlled by Canadians, is
essential to the cultural development of Canadians."[31]
Financial assistance has now been offered by the federal government to the publishing industry and also indirectly to Canadian authors.[32] In discussions of these issues Pelletier has always stressed the importance of both
"publishing and the author" and "publishing and the public."[33]
It is clear from these studies and reports that Canadians have always considered communications and mass media
to be vital to the economic, political, and sociocultural
identity of their nation. Canadian control of, and a strong
Canadian presence in, the mass media has therefore been advocated.

NOTES

1. Foreign Direct Investment in Canada (Ottawa: Information Canada, 1972), pp. 291-98.
    2. Ibid., p. 291.

11

3. "The Broadcasting Act," <u>Revised Statutes of Canada 1970</u> (Ottawa: Queen's Printer, 1970), Chap. B-11.

4. "Broadcasting Act, Direction to the Canadian Radio-Television Commission," <u>The Canada Gazette</u>, 105, no. 2, SOR/71-73 P.C. 1971-73 (Ottawa: Queen's Printer, 1971), 86-87.

5. <u>Report of the Royal Commission on Publications</u> (Ottawa: Queen's Printer, 1961).

6. <u>Report of the Special Senate Committee on Mass Media</u> (Ottawa: Queen's Printer, 1970).

7. <u>The Image</u> (Ann Arbor: University of Michigan Press, 1956), p. 125.

8. J. Porter, <u>Vertical Mosaic</u> (Toronto: University of Toronto Press, 1965), pp. 457-90.

9. See I. A. Litvak, C. J. Maule, and R. D. Robinson, <u>Dual Loyalty: Canadian-U.S. Business Arrangements</u> (Toronto: McGraw-Hill, 1971), pp. 98-111.

10. Royal Commission, op. cit., p. 4.

11. Ibid.

12. Ibid., p. 6.

13. Ibid., pp. 6-7.

14. Ibid., pp. 70-71.

15. Ibid., pp. 68-69.

16. Senate Committee, op. cit., vol. 1, p. 153.

17. (Ottawa: King's Printer, 1929), p. 6.

18. (Ottawa: King's Printer, 1951), p. 28.

19. Ibid., p. 61.

20. Ibid., p. 18.

21. Ibid., p. 24.

22. <u>Report of the Royal Commission on Broadcasting</u> (Ottawa: Queen's Printer, 1957), p. 9.

23. House of Commons Standing Committee on Broadcasting, Films and Assistance to the Arts, <u>Report of the Committee on Broadcasting</u> (Ottawa: Queen's Printer, 1965), p. 20.

24. House of Commons Standing Committee on Broadcasting, Films and Assistance to the Arts, <u>Report on the White Paper on Broadcasting 1966</u> (Ottawa: Queen's Printer, 1967), p. 4.

25. "The Broadcasting Act," op. cit.

26. <u>Annual Report</u> (Ottawa: Queen's Printer, 1969-1970), p. 5.

27. Ibid., p. 6.

28. <u>Annual Report</u> (Ottawa: Queen's Printer, 1970-1971), p. 7.

29. "The 25 Hour Week," speech to the Ottawa Canadian Club, March 9, 1971, p. 5.

30. <u>First Interim Report</u> (Toronto: Government of Ontario, March 23, 1971), p. 1.
31. "Statement on Book Publishing Policy," notes for
a speech to the Annual Meeting of Federal Cultural Agencies,
Montreal, February 11, 1972, p. 7.
32. Ibid., pp. 8-11.
33. "Canadian Publishing--Instrument of Culture,"
speech delivered to Consultation 2: Publishing Conference,
Ottawa, March 1, 1971, p. 2; and notes for a speech entitled
"Publishing--A Cultural Approach," delivered to Consultation
2: Edition Conference, Ottawa, March 2, 1971, p. 3.

2

HISTORICAL BACKGROUND, 1867-1960

1867-1929

Debate over foreign periodicals has been a part of the
Canadian scene since Confederation. Although the specific
issues have altered from time to time, the main content of
the debate has revolved around the ways in which American
periodicals may adversely affect Canada and Canadians. At
first, the main cultural and economic issues involved (1)
the need to retain British-Canadian traditions; (2) the
effect low-class American magazines might have on the values
and attitudes of Canadians, particularly young Canadians;
(3) the danger that Canadian readers would be led to emi-
grate to the United States; and (4) the effects of Canadian
economic policies on Canadian-owned periodicals that com-
peted with U.S. periodicals. The forces of patriotism,
puritanism, and economic self-interest were allied in their
concern.

However, the Canadian attitude toward U.S. periodicals
was only one part of the Canadians' general attitude toward
the United States. In the pre-Confederation period and in
the immediate post-Confederation years, Canadians were most
interested in the American political process and the effects
this process had on morality in the United States. Their
views were summed up by Sir Wilfrid Laurier in 1905 as follows:

> We live by the side of a nation . . . for which
> I have the greatest admiration, but whose exam-
> ple I would not take in everything, in whose
> schools for fear that Christian dogmas in which
> all do not believe might be taught, Christian

morals are not taught. When I compare these two
countries, when I compare Canada with the United
States, when I compare the states of the two
nations, when I think upon their future, when I
observe the social condition of civil society in
each of them and when I observe in this country
of ours, a total absence of lynchings and an
almost total absence of divorces and murders, for
my part, I thank heaven that we are living in a
country where the young children of the land are
taught Christian morals and Christian dogmas.
Either the American system is wrong or the
Canadian system is wrong. For my part I say and
I say it without hesitation. Time will show
that we are in the right, and in this instance as
in many others, I have an abiding faith in the
institutions of my own country.[1]

These Canadian views were not the result of careful
observation of the facts, and they revealed as much about
Canadians as they do about Americans:

On the whole, the judgments of Canadians upon
American political phenomena were not judgments
at all, in any rational sense, but rather were
ritualistic expressions of deeply held assump-
tions, responses triggered by danger signals
from the south that their political culture had
conditioned them to recognize.[2]

Their picture of the United States was a projec-
tion of their own fears and emotions, of their
sense of living in a hostile world, of their
anxiety for their own survival, and of their un-
certainties about their special place in North
America.[3]

The 1920s saw increasing concern over cultural influences from the United States. In this period the general
influence on Canada of the United Kingdom was waning and
that of the United States was rising. Canadians reacted by
emphasizing the need to cling to British values, by attempting to promote "things Canadian," and by being generally
defensive regarding the United States. For example, in
support of British values,

Canon Cody of St. Paul's, Toronto, preached that
the genius of the British people had been granted

by God and that it was to the credit of Britons
that they set out to share their boon with back-
ward peoples.[4]

In keeping with the urge to develop things Canadian
was the founding of the Canadian Authors Association in
1921, the Canadian Bookman in 1919, the Canadian Forum in
1920, the Dalhousie Review in 1921, the McGill Fortnightly
in 1925, and the Canadian Mercury in 1928; following the
Royal Commission on Radio Broadcasting, which reported in
1929, the forerunner of the Canadian Broadcasting Corporation was formed in 1932. The National Film Board was formed
in 1939. During the 1920s Maclean's Magazine had a policy
of publishing nonfiction articles only if they related to
a Canadian topic, and even stated that it did not intend
"to practice any other spellings than those which are
thoroughly Canadian."[5]

A further concern at this time was the fact that the
Canadian media relied heavily on American wire services
for their news. Noting this situation, Arthur Meighen
stated, "We know that the news that comes to Canada filters
through New York, indeed it is censored from the American
standpoint."[6] This concern with the failure to obtain a
Canadian view of events was to arise again in connection
with Time's presence in Canada in the 1960s.

The flavor of the 1920s can be found in the letters
of W. L. Grant, who wrote to J. W. Defoe,

While I do not think that there is any danger of
our being politically absorbed by the United
States, there is a danger of our being "Ameri-
canized" socially.[7]

and in the writings of Professor F. Underhill,

If then we are to save ourselves from that ultimate
cultural absorption into the United States . . .
it must not be done by harking back to our British inheritance but by going forward and creating a Canadian culture of our own.[8]

It is interesting to note that French-Canadian nation-
alists were more concerned with the cultural impact of the
American cinema than with the printed media and radio.
Language provided a barrier to print and radio, but there
was still a visual influence from the cinema.[9] This attitude was to prevail in later years, with French Canadians

being less concerned over the periodical issue than English Canadians.

In this early period the issue of copyright worked to the advantage of British and American publishers and authors and to the disadvantage of those in Canada.

> Canadian copyright was based on the Imperial Copyright Act of 1842, as amended in 1847. This forbade the reprinting of British books in the colonies but permitted the import of American reprints on payment of a duty of 12 1/2 per cent as compensation to British authors in lieu of royalties. Moreover an American author, by establishing temporary residence in Canada and sending a few advance copies of his latest book to England for "first publication", could obtain full protection under the Imperial Act against the reprinting of his work in Canada. A Canadian author's copyright in Great Britain, however, was forfeited if the original form of publication in Canada was deemed to be inferior to British standards.[10]

This situation was corrected partially by a Canadian copyright act in 1875.

The political union of Canada in 1867 did provide a stimulus to the native periodical industry, affording it the opportunity to give expression and form to the elusive concept of Canadian nationality. The economic motives underlying Confederation were of paramount consideration, and in many ways political union was viewed as a structural means of promoting commercial interests. Greater financial resources became available and the population expanded. Railways linked the provinces of the new far-flung nation, thereby increasing the potential for communications, and under the umbrella of Prime Minister Macdonald's national tariff policy, industry mushroomed. The chances for survival of Canadian magazines should have increased substantially, because the readership audience was greatly enlarged through the creation of a national market and the rising industrialists needed advertising media.

However, the Canadian periodical industry never really flourished; from the outset, precarious and short-lived ventures were the rule. Propinquity to the United States, a common North American language and culture, and a relatively sparse and dispersed population posed formidable obstacles to the development of a distinct and flourishing Canadian periodical industry.

17

In addition to the overwhelming number of American magazines that dominated the market, Canadian publishers experienced two major disadvantages.[11] First, Canadian periodical publishers paid a duty on all the raw materials used
in production; this meant that it was cheaper to establish
publishing houses across the border and export to Canada.
Second, competing American magazines enjoyed tremendous
economies of scale because their overhead costs could be
spread over a large domestic circulation. The additional
cost of producing the same magazine for Canadian readers
was small compared to the cost for Canadian magazine publishers, who seemed unable or unwilling to crack the U.S.
market. Thus it appeared to Canadians that U.S. magazines
were dumped in Canada for the benefit of U.S. producers and
advertisers.

Canadian publishers pressured several governments for
remedial action, and by 1922 they had articulated three
specific demands: first, that the present tariff on printed
and advertising matter be applied to advertisements contained in foreign magazines and periodicals; second, that
the government should apply the tariff to paper entering
Canada in the form of finished magazines; and third, that
all duties on paper, ink, engravings, and other raw materials used in magazine production should be removed.[12]
Such protection for the Canadian magazine industry was certainly not a new idea; every previous government had had to
deal with it, but no government had yet been prepared to impose the duty.

Canadian magazines found a dedicated and well-informed
advocate in the person of H. C. Hocken, a former newspaper
reporter and editor and a Unionist member of Parliament
from Toronto West since 1917, who persistently crusaded for
the cause of Canadian periodicals.* The issue was first in-

---

*Horatio Clarence Hocken was born on October 12, 1857.
He began work in the mechanical department of the Toronto
Globe at the age of 16; he became a reporter with the _News_
and was promoted to chief editor. Hocken left this position in 1902 to purchase an interest in the St. Thomas
Journal, but after one year he left and went back to work
on the _News_. He quit this job once again in 1905 and purchased the _Sentinel_, the official organ of the Orange Order
in North America. In 1907 he was elected to the Toronto
Board of Control and became the mayor in 1912. At the end
of 1914 he voluntarily retired. He was elected to the
House of Commons in 1917 as a Unionist and remained in the

troduced in the House in 1922,[14] and in 1923 the following Hocken resolution received unanimous approval: "That in the opinion of this House, it is desirable that measures should be adopted to encourage the publication of Canadian magazines and periodicals."[15] This gesture of sympathy was stripped of its token significance soon afterward by the 1923 budget of Finance Minister Fielding, which increased the sales tax on raw materials from 4.5 percent to 6 percent.[16]

The plea for government intervention to curb the massive inflow of American magazines rested on seven points. It was argued:

1. That the great bulk of United States magazines consisted of salacious literature that dissipated the morals of Canadian youth. Hocken, in quasi-evangelical fashion, warned that there was

> an enormous flood of literature of the most objectionable character coming in from the United States . . . [and] produced for the sole purpose of appealing to the most vicious traits of humanity.[17]

In like vein, the Vancouver _Morning Star_ preached that the

> mentality and morale of impressionable young Canadians, which should be kept clean and apart to their own land, is being merged in the reeking gas cloud of the lower Americanism. . . . Something should be done . . . to dam this trash which is flowing over the border.[18]

2. That American publications were mainly responsible for Canada's "brain drain" by depicting the United States as a land of unlimited promise, higher wages, better living conditions, and "good times," and thereby attracting misguided Canadian youth. Hubbs, the member for Prince Edward County, contended that American publications were " . . . doing nothing more nor less than educating our boys and girls to become citizens of the United States."[19] While

House until 1930 as the Conservative member from Toronto West Centre. Hocken was also a member of Toronto's Albany Club and the Toronto Board of Trade. In 1933 he was called to the Canadian Senate.[13]

Hocken noted, "the very children of Canada are being led away across the border, in their mind at least, by a new Pied Piper in the guise of the cheap American magazine."[20]

3. That United States publications, especially those of the Hearst Syndicate, often expressed opinions repugnant to British sentiment in Canada.[21]

4. That United States magazines posed an economic threat because of the substantial volume of advertising they conveyed, which attracted customers that would otherwise buy from Canadian manufacturers.[22] It was contended that this resulted in the outflow of large sums of Canadian dollars and placed Canadian industrialists at a serious disadvantage, since they could not afford the advertising rates demanded by such publications. Further, this American advertising entered Canada duty-free because it was contained in magazines, thus avoiding the advertising tax of 15 cents a pound.

5. That the Canadian magazine industry was fighting a losing battle for its very survival and desperately needed protection or assistance of some sort so as to equalize its competitive position in relation to foreign publications.[23] Hocken maintained that the imposition of a tariff on American magazines and the elimination of taxes on the raw materials used by the Canadian publications industry were the two essential concessions.[24] It should be noted that the morality question concerning the entry of undesirable literature was distinguished from the question of magazines loaded with advertising: the former should be dealt with by excluding entry altogether, while a tariff would be appropriate for the latter.

6. That magazines are crucial vehicles in the generation and dissemination of national sentiment and therefore deserve special consideration apart from strictly commercial calculations.[25] The steady inflow of American literature was claimed to be sapping Canada's national life; therefore the magazine industry was said to merit protection for the sake of Canadian culture and nationality.*

7. That Canadian publishers cannot sell U.S. circulation to Canadian advertisers because the latter are not interested in doing business in the U.S. market.[27]

_____

*This was not perceived to be a problem in Quebec, for as Henri Bourassa (Labelle) pointed out, the French language shielded the Quebecois from the penetration of Americanism.[26]

In sum, these arguments represent a wide interest in economic protectionism and cultural nationalism that would reappear when the argument on cultural identity formed the basis of the 1960 Report of the Royal Commission on Publications.[28]

Interest groups such as the Toronto Women's Liberal Association, the Imperial Order of the Daughters of the Empire, the Canadian Manufacturers Association, the Association of Canadian Clubs, and others also voiced concern over the overwhelming number of American magazines found on Canadian magazine stalls.[29] These and many others wanted the entry of American magazines curbed, but usually for reasons other than the promotion of a healthy Canadian magazine industry. Genuine concern for the health of Canadian culture and the native magazine industry was one motive for demanding restrictions on the importation of U.S. periodicals, but many groups advocated restrictive measures for other reasons. For example, the Toronto Women's Liberal Association probably reacted quite indignantly to the "girly" magazines entering Canada; the Daughters of the Empire were instinctively set aghast by any traces of anti-imperial sentiment; while the Canadian Manufacturers Association did not cherish the idea of Canadians purchasing from manufacturers across the border, who often offered similar products at much cheaper prices.

These issues evoked rather intense responses from the foreign periodicals lobby, and such hallowed principles as freedom of the press and freedom of readership selection were immediately invoked to ward off any prohibitive action against foreign publications that might have been contemplated. G. W. Kyte, a Liberal member, charged Hocken with endeavoring to "protect the people against selecting their literature" and stated that, "I do not think the reading public of Canada ought to be penalized on account of their [the Canadian periodicals'] failure."[30] J. Evans, a Progressive member from Saskatoon, argued that the advocates of protection were really little concerned about the nature of the reading material or the unfair competition imposed on Canadian magazines, that their real target was the advertisements contained in American magazines.[31] However, Fielding, the Liberal Finance Minister,* while sympathetic

---

*William Stevens Fielding was Minister of Finance in the Liberal government from 1896 to 1911 and from 1921 to 1925. The fact that in 1864 Fielding became connected with the Halifax Morning Chronicle, ultimately working his way

to the plight of Canadian periodicals, felt that public
opinion on the whole was opposed to the imposition of a
customs duty on U.S. magazines.[33]

Apparently the government regarded itself as quite
capable of dealing with foreign periodicals under existing
legislation,[34] since advertisements placed in magazines
entered Canada duty-free and the Minister of Customs had
the discretionary power to impose a tax on all magazines
containing advertisements by giving the proper definition
to certain items of the tariff. The Customs Department
maintained, however, that it was not administratively feasi-
ble to separate reading from advertising material--even
though this was being done in the United States. Moreover,
since many American magazines were probably being sold in
Canada for less than their true value, a dumping duty
could also have been imposed. Because the Customs Department classified magazines as unbound, they entered Canada
duty-free under Item 184 of the tariff; if magazines were
properly classified as bound, then Item 169 of the tariff
would have applied and a duty of 25 percent would have been
levied. Further, the Customs Department could censor any
material it deemed to be salacious.[35] The Postal Department could also help, and the Postmaster-General, P. J.
Venoit, was urged to devise some means of securing revenues
from the massive influx of American magazines. In 1927
Venoit delighted supporters of the Canadian magazine industry when he promised that "a thorough investigation will
be made with a view to devising some scheme by which we
can give greater protection to our newspapers and periodicals in competition with American publications."[36] The
Speaker of the House took the liberty of interjecting with,
"I hope the Postmaster-General and the Minister of Customs
will deal with this matter in a drastic way. We must protect our youth."[37] Any expectation of protection because
of this promise was dispelled a week later, when Venoit
announced that his remark should be limited to the moral
implications of American magazines.[38] The government, pre-
occupied with the issue of licentious reading material,
failed to direct its attention to the issue of the survival
of Canadian culture in a prosperous periodical press.

––––––––––––––––––––

up to managing editor, plus the fact that he served as a
Nova Scotia correspondent for the Toronto <u>Globe</u>, probably
help explain his sympathetic response to the Canadian magazine publishers' demands.[32]

22

By 1927, however, some signs of concern and some actual assistance were forthcoming. A 1926-27 postal amendment resulted in a slight reduction in postal rates for Canadian magazines.[39] At about this time the Tariff Advisory Board entered the debate and initiated a consideration of the imposition of a duty on foreign magazines, for which Canadian publishers were pressing.[40] Shortly thereafter a ruling of the board reclassified some magazines under Item 169 of the tariff as bound material. Fiction magazines such as Argosy, Western Stories, and Real Romances, which had previously come under Item 184 (unbound material), were now dutiable. At this time the Magazine Publishing Association (MPA) independently surveyed public and parliamentary opinion and found such opinion strongly opposed to any tax on reading material.[41] From then on the MPA ceased advocating the imposition of a duty or any other protective measure, and instead demanded simply parity in production costs with foreign competitors.

In 1928 the government finally made an effort to meet MPA wishes and granted a drawback of 80 percent of the duty on printing paper and some printing material. By 1929 Canadian publishers were demanding a 99 percent drawback on printing plant and machinery, art work, and engravings, and the removal of the sales tax. Thus, by the end of this decade Canadian magazine publishers were no longer claiming tariff protection, which they were not likely to get from the Liberal government of Mackenzie King, but were pressuring to have their raw materials available on a duty-free basis.

THE 1931 TARIFF AND
FOREIGN ENTRY

The 1930 Conservative electoral victory ushered into power the party that had fathered the tariff and was thus traditionally inclined toward protection. The 1931 budget proposed that magazines and periodicals be subject to a specific duty of 15 cents a pound under the general tariff, plus a 1 percent excise tax. Scientific, educational, and religious magazines were excluded from the tax.[42] It was then realized that under this proposed procedure the duty would fall more heavily on better-class magazines, such as The Saturday Evening Post and The Atlantic Monthly, than on the salacious variety of literature, which was generally lighter in weight. Consequently the duty was altered to make advertising content determine the rate of tax. Magazines with 20 percent or less advertising content were allowed free entry; those with advertising content up to 30 percent paid two cents a copy; and those with greater than 30 percent advertising content paid five cents a copy.[43] It was also agreed that religious, educational, scientific, philanthropic, agricultural, labor, and fraternal publications should enjoy free entry.

Prime Minister Bennett defended the tax on the grounds that its intent was basically to obtain some revenue from advertisements in foreign publications and was motivated in no way by a desire to shield industry or manufacturers.[44] It was hoped, however, that the tax would have the ancillary effect of discouraging the entry of undesirable literature and of easing the competitive glut of American magazines, thereby enhancing the competitive position of Canadian periodicals.

Mackenzie King perceived the motives behind this tax less naively than Bennett and deplored any tax that tampered with the free flow of ideas.[45] He went on to warn of possible U.S. reprisals, such as loss of opportunities for Canadian writers in American magazines; restrictions on pulp and paper exports to the United States; and a possible cutback in the tourist trade, since Americans might experience difficulty in obtaining home magazines. He argued that the tax would undoubtedly mean higher prices for American periodicals and possibly harder times for many who were already impoverished by the depressed state of the economy. The real motivating force behind the tax, he said, was the desire of Canadian manufacturers to exclude foreign advertising material.

> It is a further restriction of trade, it is again
> an effort to further the interests of a particular
> class at the expense of the great body of consum-
> ers. . . . I think that is the real explanation
> of [the tax].[46]

Mackenzie King was probably quite close to the truth; the legislation undoubtedly resulted from the activity of certain Canadian magazine publishers in conjunction with the Canadian Manufacturers Association; but the facts are unclear. Bennett readily admitted his apprehension over the entry into Canada of magazines advertising commodities at lower prices and extolling American values.[47] Notwithstanding, he insisted that the tax was strictly for revenue purposes and aimed at assisting Canadian magazines, while King protested that the tax was just one more protectionist device intended to limit competition rather than promote Canadian culture.

The reaction of publishers to the tax is also of interest. Hugh Maclean, president of Hugh C. Maclean Publications,* thought that the tax would provide a much needed stimulus to Canadian magazines, while relieving Canadian manufacturers of the necessity of advertising in American magazines.[49] H. N. Moore, editor of Maclean's Magazine, insisted that the Maclean's organization had made no attempt to secure such a duty and was not consulted by the government about it.[50] The Canadian Wholesale Newspaper Association presented its views to the government and claimed that it had been assured that such a tax would not be imposed.[51] J. Atkin, secretary of the National Magazine and Periodical Association, declined comment at the time. A small delegation of Canadian publishers from Toronto, Montreal, and Winnipeg demanded further concessions and urged the Commissioner of Customs to tax American Sunday newspapers containing magazine sections.[52] A meeting was arranged between the Minister of National Revenue and Canadian newsdealers, along with United States representatives including Charles Lucas of the American Magazine Publishers Association.[53] Also, a letter written by B. C. Duffy, chairman of the American Magazine Advertisers Association's committee on magazines, and circulated among U.S. magazine publishers stated that

> the tax of 15 cents per pound will be placed on all U.S. periodicals entering Canada as of July 1, 1931. . . . This tariff action on magazines was brought about by the activity of certain Canadian magazine publishers together with the Canadian Manufacturers Association. Printing in Canada would overcome the obstacle of the tariff, but few Canadian plants are equipped to handle the volume. If the magazines allow this tariff to interfere with their circulation it is an injustice to American manufacturers and advertisers.[54]

---

*The list of publications of Hugh C. Maclean Publications Ltd. included Canadian Magazine. Maclean was also president of Maclean Building Reports Ltd., which published daily advance information about engineering and building projects, and of the Muskoka Lakes Navigation and Hotel Co., which operated steamers and hotels.[48]

But in the end the legislation was altered only slightly from that originally proposed.

Prime Minister Bennett's tariff apparently helped the Canadian magazine industry, because by 1935 the circulation of American magazines in Canada decreased by 62 percent while Canadian magazine circulation increased by 64 percent.[55] But after 1931 foreign competition assumed a new form, for it was now deemed to be advantageous to U.S. publishers to jump the tariff wall and establish operations in Canada; by 1932 there were 47 subsidiaries of fiction magazines publishing their Canadian circulation in Canada. (See Table 2.1.)

These magazines still enjoyed a tremendous competitive advantage over Canadian-owned magazines with regard to edi-

TABLE 2.1

Fiction Magazines in Canada, 1932

Ace High	Love Story
Aces	Master Detective
Action Stories	Railroad Man's Magazine
Adventure	Ranch Romances
All Story	Rangeland Love Story
Argosy	Short Story
Ballyhoo	Sport Story
Battle Aces	Sweetheart Stories
Battle Stories	Thrilling Detective Tales
Blue Book	Triple X
Clues	True Confessions
College Life	True Detective
Complete Detective Novel	True Experience
Magazine	True Romances
Complete Stories	True Story Magazine
Cowboy Stories	War Aces
Detective Fiction	War Birds
Detective Story	West
Dime Detective Magazine	Western Rangers
Dream World	Western Romances
Family Journal	Western Story
Far East	Wild West Stories and Com-
Fight Stories	plete Novel Magazine
Film Fun	Wings
Lariat Story	

Source: Hansard, February 25, 1932, p. 507.

torial expenses: the parent companies simply shipped the
lithograph plates for the Canadian editions into Canada
duty-free. At the same time that the unwelcome publications
were recapturing their Canadian market, better-class magazines such as The Atlantic Monthly, Harper's Magazine, and
the Literary Digest actually suffered a reduction in circulation.[56]

The Liberals, who had vehemently opposed the imposition of the tax, had their chance to remove the protective
legislation when they returned to power in 1935. The question arose in connection with the Canada-U.S. Trade Agreement, which proposed to repeal the Canadian tax on foreign
magazines for the three-year duration of the treaty.* Because Canadian magazines were granted free entry into the
United States the American government demanded reciprocal
arrangements. What influence American publishers exerted
is not revealed, but it is reasonable to suppose that it
was quite significant.

Mackenzie King now appeared to perceive the periodical
issue as basically an economic and commercial problem and
not as one of cultural and nationalistic import. He accused
Canadian publishers of raising the cultural bogey that unless tariff barriers were erected to check the entry of
American publications the Canadian character would be seriously jeopardized.[58] He dismissed any argument founded on
cultural grounds as "obviously far-fetched" and obstinately
reasserted that he would not place any restrictions on the
free flow of ideas.**

During the Trade Agreement debate the opposition warned
of the threat to Canadian culture posed by the deluge of
foreign periodicals void of any Canadian viewpoint, the
derogatory effect upon Canadian values of magazines devoted
to "cheap sensationalism and pallid pornography," and the
disadvantages imposed upon Canadian manufacturers.

_____

*This treaty, which was signed in Washington on Novem-
ber 15, 1935, proposed numerous changes in the tariff, all
in the nature of reductions. It would take effect pending
the acquiescence of Parliament. This treaty marked the
first reciprocal trade agreement between Canada and the
United States to become law since Confederation, although
the Liberals under Alexander Mackenzie had negotiated one
in 1874 and Laurier likewise in 1911. The only previous
U.S.-Canada trade agreement was in force from 1854 to 1866.[57]

**This attitude was criticized by Senator O'Leary during
the hearings of the Royal Commission on Publications in
1960-61.

The importation of U.S. magazines quickly increased after the tax was removed. These figures are cited:[59]

Year	Value of Imported U.S. Magazines
1935	$2,625,000
1936	4,037,000
1937	5,900,000

Repeal of the tax led to the withdrawal of numerous American magazine subsidiaries: 52 had left by 1937.[60] The names of the departing subsidiaries and their withdrawal dates are not available, but Table 2.1 lists 47 U.S. magazines that had set up Canadian operations by 1932, and it is probably safe to assume that most of these left Canada shortly after the repeal of the tax. The exodus commenced shortly after the announcement of the Canada-U.S. Trade Agreement in February 1936 and was fairly complete by the end of that year. Within a period of five years Canadian government policy had managed first to create and then to break the custom of publishing foreign magazines in Canada,[61] without having much effect on the circulation of foreign periodicals in the country.

The few statistics that are available for this early period show a fair number of births and deaths of magazines. (See Table 4.1.) Up to 1950 more seem to have been born than died.

CANADIAN EDITIONS OF TIME AND READER'S DIGEST

From the time of the Trade Agreement debate until the mid-1950s, there was little political discussion centering on the interests of the Canadian magazine industry (see Figure 2.1). In 1939 the Liberal government did meet a previous demand of Canadian publishers by imposing a ban on the importation of weekend newspapers printed in the United States.[62] The war effort monopolized public interest but, at times, certain U.S. magazines incurred public censure by expressing opinions critical of the allied effort.[63] In general, the publications issue remained dormant, and no reprisals against U.S. publications were entertained by the Canadian government.

In 1943, Reader's Digest became incorporated in Canada, and in the same year Time began printing its special Canadian edition in Chicago. This was a new type of competition,

FIGURE 2.1

Profile of Parliamentary Activity Regarding the Publications Issue

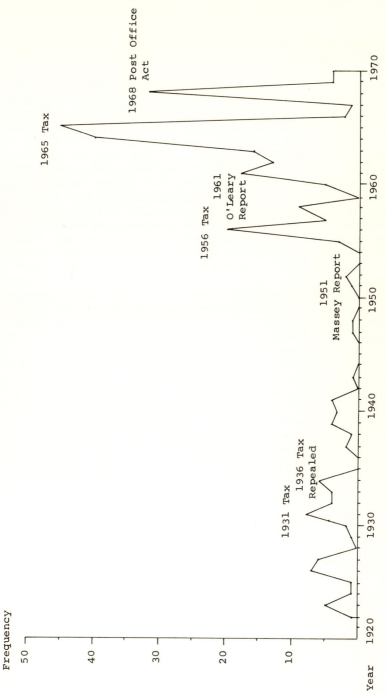

Source: Tabulated by the authors from the number of references to the publications issue occurring in the House of Commons Debates for the years 1920 to 1970.

29

masquerading as Canadian and not merely an outlet for over-flow circulation.

Although the <u>Report of the Royal Commission on National Development in the Arts, Letters and Sciences</u> (called the Massey Report), which was tabled in 1951, did not express concern for the periodical press officially and offered no formal recommendations in this regard, it did recognize that periodicals alone can "be regarded as really important factors or influences in the formation and development of national understanding."[64] The Royal Commission's terms of reference stated, "It is in the national interest to give encouragement to institutions which add to the variety and richness of Canadian life, rural as well as urban."[65]

In a study prepared for the Royal Commission it was concluded that tariffs would be a barrier against ideas and intellectual stimulation and that subsidies and subventions would be politically suspect.[66] The study argued that the press could best be helped by policies that reduced the costs of capital equipment and raw materials and improved postal efficiency and lowered mailing costs. The commission's report stated: "We are informed that the important Canadian magazines . . . manage to survive and even to flourish although American periodicals outsell them by more than two to one."[67] The commissioners were impressed by the fact that Canadian periodicals neither desired nor requested any protective measures, apart from the demand they were still making for a 99 percent drawback in the duties on paper.[68] But by 1956 the prospects for survival of Canadian magazines had deteriorated, and the industry began demanding protection as it had done until the late 1920s.*

Requests for assistance grew in intensity after 1952.[70] The Liberals under Prime Minister St. Laurent had become much more concerned about the health of Canadian magazines for the following reasons.

First, the proportion of Canadian to non-Canadian magazines in circulation had fallen steadily, so that only one-fifth of all consumer magazines read in Canada were of Canadian origin;[71] the share of the Canadian market obtained by all U.S. magazines, including special editions, had risen from 67 percent in 1948 to 80 percent in 1954.

---

*It is not certain exactly when Canadian publishers began pressing for tariff protection once again. Early in 1956 the Periodical Press Association appeared before the Gordon Commission on Canada's economic prospects, but their brief did not request tariff protection.[69]

Second, general interest magazines in Canada were generally financial disasters, and only a few remained, including _Time_ and _Reader's Digest_ as well as _Canadian Home Journal_, _Canadian Homes and Gardens_, _Chatelaine_, _Maclean's_, _Liberty_, _Mayfair_, _Saturday Night_, _La Revue Moderne_, _La Revue Populaire_, and _Le Samedi_.[72]

Third, special Canadian editions of U.S. magazines were drastically cutting into the financial foundations of the Canadian magazine industry. In 1948, _Time_ and _Reader's Digest_ accounted for 18 percent of the total advertising revenues of these twelve major magazines; by 1955 their share had increased to 37 percent.[73] Moreover, several U.S. women's magazines had special Canadian editions that also siphoned off a share of the advertisers' dollars, including _Family Circle_, _Woman's Day_, _Everywoman's_ and _Parent's Magazine_. These special editions provided fierce competition, as is evidenced by their share of advertising revenue, since their editorial costs were substantially lower than for Canadian magazines. It was also believed that two other well-known magazines published in the United States were planning Canadian editions and that an established publisher of trade papers was set to invade the business publications field in Canada.*

In light of these developments it became clear that failure to grant assistance would assuredly result in the eventual disappearance of several of the few remaining Canadian general circulation magazines.

In bringing down the budget in March of 1956, Liberal Finance Minister Harris prefaced his proposed tax with the following words:

> We have been considering this problem for some time, and we have decided that in this field, very exceptional measures can be justified--measures that certainly could not be justified in connection with any ordinary line of business.[75]

The Liberal government was thus converted to the view expressed in the Massey Report and first uttered in the House back in 1922, that native publications are essential to Canada's national life. The budget speech went on to propose a 20 percent tax on all advertising contained in Canada or abroad, in English or in French, to become effective

---

*Supposedly, _Newsweek_, _Business Week_, and _Better Homes and Gardens_ were planning to enter Canada.[74]

on January 1, 1957.[76] _Time_, _Reader's Digest_, _Woman's Day_, _Everywoman's_, _Better Living_, _Canadian Farm Chemicals_, _Cleaning and Laundry World_, _Canadian Office_, _Parent's Magazine_, and _Family Circle_ would be affected by the tax.[77] The Liberals contended that the intent of the tax was solely to try to balance production costs of Canadian magazines against the special editions of foreign magazines.

The Conservatives opposed this tax proposal with outraged zeal, which more than equaled that exhibited by the Liberals during the 1931 tax debate. During the debate the following arguments against the tax became discernible:

Tariff protection is unnecessary; Canadian magazines could compete favorably if they were guided by better management and if they presented a better product.[78]

Canadian magazines are not in serious trouble. The "long-run continuation of Canadian magazines is not in any jeopardy whatsoever."[79] "This is not a depressed Canadian industry. On the contrary, it is a thriving, prosperous example of Canadian enterprise at its competitive best."[80]

If this tax forces _Time_ and _Reader's Digest_ to pull out of Canada there will be a substantial economic loss to the country.

The 20 percent rate of taxation is a completely arbitrary figure and bears no relation to the equality of competition.

Time and _Reader's Digest_ may simply increase their advertising rates by 20 percent. If Canadian advertisers decide to stick with these magazines then there will be a debilitating cutback in the advertising revenue available to Canadian magazines. Moreover, Canadian magazines are really incapable of meeting the demands of these advertisers, and advertising revenue will simply go to the other competing media.[81]

The tax is a form of censorship and an interference with the reading habits of Canadians. It singles out and discriminates against 9 special editions out of a total of 100 general circulation magazines imported to Canada from the United States.[82]

The tax is designed to penalize the nondomestic part of an industry in order to divert revenues to domestic industry. It is basically a punitive tax imposed for political reasons.[83] The government has been accused of selling out the economy to Americans; this tax is just its token expression of readiness to resist U.S. penetration.

The tax could shake the faith of investors because of the inconsistency of government policy toward foreign investment.[84]

W. S. Honneus, advertising director of <u>Time</u>'s international editions, termed the tax proposal as "punitive," "unbecoming," and "discriminatory." Honneus argued that <u>Time</u> helped strengthen Canadian advertising and the Canadian magazine industry by encouraging advertisers to include a larger proportion of magazine advertising in their budgets. <u>Time</u> also argued that the failings of Canadian magazines were not the result of the presence of U.S. publications but that the Canadian public merely preferred magazines of "superior quality."[85]

Reader's Digest probably reserved its comments for the private ear of government; on March 21, 1956 the <u>Globe and Mail</u> and Toronto <u>Star</u> simply observed that <u>Reader's Digest</u> had no immediate comment. However, on March 23 the New York <u>Times</u> recorded the remarks of Walter Hitesman, Jr., managing director of <u>Reader's Digest</u> (Canada). Hitesman assailed the "discriminatory" tax and asserted that "precedents such as this tax on advertising can be extremely dangerous and have far-reaching implications on the freedom of the press itself." He went on to emphasize that <u>Reader's Digest</u> was a "Canadian magazine, printed and published in Canada and paying its full share of Canadian taxes."[87] <u>Reader's Digest</u> also filed a suit in the Supreme Court of Quebec contesting the legislation's validity on the grounds that such legislation was <u>ultra vires</u> of Parliament's jurisdiction. Reader's Digest, which withheld payment of the tax, was in turn sued by the federal government.[88]

F. S. Chalmers, president of Maclean-Hunter, commented upon the fact that the government has "recognized the importance of Canada's own native literature in the development of our national economy and our spirit of nationhood."[89] Chalmers also expected that "in due course the Government will act upon the problems of the tidal wave of American magazines that pour in each year."[90] However, Stuart Keate, publisher of the Victoria <u>Daily News</u>, later remarked that his newspaper was one of about 75 in Canada that entered strong editorial protests against the 1956 tax.[91]

The tax really was not in effect long enough to have a telling impact on the magazine industry, since the Conservatives replaced the Liberal government and repealed the tax in June 1958: $498,645.78 had been collected under the tax in the 12-month period prior to its repeal June 18, 1958.[92]

Six months after the repeal of the tax, five new Canadian editions began to publish. <u>Family Circle</u>, having absorbed <u>Everywoman's</u> and appearing as <u>Everywoman's Family</u>

Circle, resumed publication of its Canadian edition, which it had discontinued with the advent of the tax. Argosy and True began publishing Canadian editions, and TV Guide announced the inauguration of an Ontario edition. Further, Popular Mechanics, The Saturday Evening Post, and Life began indulging in split-run advertising.

More unsettling was evidence around this time that the exportation of magazines was being encouraged as a matter of U.S. government policy. This evidence is found in a 1959 U.S. Post Office announcement of reductions in the postal rates of magazines mailed to foreign countries.

> In view of growing world acceptance of American published materials, and the desire of Americans to encourage their influence abroad (international postage rates will be lowered). . . . By this new move we will be keeping increases moderate enough to encourage continued growth of the world market for printed materials which spread American ideals, culture and facts abroad.[93]

Repeal of the tax left the problem unsolved and aggravated the uncertainty of the magazine business about what the government intended to do. The well-worn issues pertaining to the problem were not rehashed in debate, but R. Bourgue, a Liberal from Outremont-St. Jean, continued to direct the House's attention to the financial burden imposed on the Post Office by the immense volume of American literature, which contributed nothing by way of revenue when mailed from the United States.[94] The flood of American magazines was also singled out as a major contributory factor to the underdevelopment of and unemployment in the graphic arts business.[95] Pressures for action existed, but the Conservatives appeared to be uncertain what measures to take. Finally, on September 16, 1960, more than two years after the repeal of the tax, Prime Minister Diefenbaker, through order-in-council, appointed a Royal Commission to investigate and suggest solutions for Canada's magazine industry.

SUMMARY

It is clear from the foregoing that the fortunes of Canadian periodicals had been discussed at length prior to the formation of the Royal Commission on Publications. There had been a mixture of arguments for and against eco-

nomic protectionism and cultural nationalism, flavored
with views about freedom of access to information and expressions of anti-Americanism. During the period up to
1960 neither the Liberal nor the Conservative party took a
consistent stand on the periodical issues on a national
level. Both parties introduced legislation that discrimi-
nated against foreign periodicals, and each argued against
the introduction of such legislation by the other.

Underlying the debate from the start was the influence
the United States had on Canada. In the words of Arthur
Meighen, "We have one neighbor and one only, and that one
an industrial colossus. . . . There is the dominating fact
that meets Canadians every morning."[96] The issue of foreign
periodicals was the issue of American periodicals, and the
measures introduced were part of the policy of "defensive
expansionism" that has characterized so much of Canadian
economic history.[97] The arguments put forward stressed
the effects of American magazines on Canadian life styles
as well as on Canadian periodicals; those arguing against
the inflow of American magazines certainly included other
than spokesmen for Canadian periodical interests.

Political influence exerted on Canadian policy toward
periodicals by American interests is difficult to document,
although it is clear that the negotiations over the Trade
Agreement of 1936 were used as a lever to repeal the tax on
foreign periodicals.

One interesting point to note is that some Canadians
seemed to believe that discouraging the sale of American
periodicals might benefit Canadian periodicals because the
advertisers might either switch to competing media or,
where possible, pay the higher price to continue advertising
in American magazines. This concern became a theme in subsequent years.

NOTES

1. House of Commons Debates, February 21, 1905, pp.
1458-59. [Hereafter referred to as Hansard.]

2. The evolution of Canadian attitudes toward the
United States in the nineteenth century is covered in S. F.
Wise and R. Craig Brown, Canada Views the United States
(Seattle: University of Washington Press, 1967), this quo-
tation is from p. 95.

3. Ibid., p. 97.

4. J. C. Weaver, "Canadians Confront American Mass
Culture, 1918-1930," paper presented to the Canadian Historical Association, Montreal, June 1972, p. 3.

5. <u>Maclean's</u>, February 15, 1927, p. 63, quoted in Weaver, op. cit., p. 11.

6. <u>Canadian Annual Review, 1921</u> (Toronto: The Canadian Review Company Ltd.), p. 217.

7. <u>W. L. Grant Papers</u>, letter of Grant to Defoe, papers held by National Archives, Ottawa, December 29, 1927.

8. F. H. Underhill, "O Canada," <u>Canadian Forum</u>, 10 (October 1929), p. 12.

9. Weaver, op. cit., p. 28.

10. H. Pearson Gundy, "Literary Publishing," in C. F. Klinck, ed., Literary History of Canada (Toronto: University of Toronto Press, 1965), pp. 183-84.

11. <u>Hansard</u>, March 5, 1923, pp. 826-56.

12. These demands were enunciated in a telegram from Canadian publishers to members of the House. Ibid, June 17, 1922, p. 3110.

13. <u>The Canadian Who's Who, 1936-37</u>; <u>The Canadian Parliamentary Guide</u>, 1930.

14. <u>Hansard</u>, June 17, 1922, p. 3109.

15. Ibid., March 5, 1923, p. 826.

16. Ibid., June 26, 1923, p. 4415.

17. <u>Hansard</u>, May 30, 1928, p. 3576.

18. Ibid., April 29, 1926, p. 2930. For a brief survey of some editorial reaction to "dirty" American literature in Canada see "Protests Against Salacious Magazines," <u>Maclean's</u>, April 15, 1938, pp. 47-48. For example, the survey included the following reaction of George Wright, columnist of the Vancouver <u>News-Herald</u>: "It is high time we called a halt to the circulation of this garbage and disposed of it in the place to which it should be relegated-- the scavenger cart or the incinerator. It is sheer hypocrisy to talk about building up a Canadian culture and giving expression to Canadian thought and Canadian ideals while this bilge is allowed to enter the country freely and be sold to every child who can beg, borrow or steal a dime for its purchase."

19. <u>Hansard</u>, May 12, 1924, p. 2012.

20. Ibid., April 29, 1926, p. 2930.

21. Ibid., March 5, 1923, p. 828.

22. Ibid., May 12, 1924, p. 2012; February 16, 1925, pp. 210-11.

23. Ibid., February 16, 1925, pp. 210-11; May 6, 1926, p. 2925.

24. Ibid., March 5, 1923, p. 833.

25. Ibid., June 17, 1922, p. 3109; March 5, 1923, pp. 828-29.

26. <u>Hansard</u>, January 12, 1926, p. 84.

27. Hearing No. 9 of the Canadian Tariff Board, February 2, 1927. These issues are also covered in H. F. Angus, ed., Canada and Her Great Neighbor (New York: Russell and Russell, 1938), pp. 152-72.

28. (Ottawa: Queen's Printer, 1961).

29. Hansard, March 5, 1923, p. 832.

30. Ibid., June 17, 1922, p. 3109.

31. Ibid., June 17, 1922, p. 3113.

32. Parliamentary Guide, 1925.

33. Ibid., June 17, 1922, pp. 3111-13; June 26, 1923, p. 4415.

34. Ibid., February 24, 1927, p. 607; April 7, 1927, pp. 2033-34.

35. For a list of publications banned from Canada, see Senate Debates, March 31, 1922, pp. 67-69. Examples of books banned were: Richard Burton, Arabian Nights (unexpurgated edition); The Confessions of a Princess (anon.); Guy de Maupassant, Always Lock the Door, The Wedding Night, and Women's Wiles; forms requesting contributions for the defense of members of the Industrial Workers of the World held in penitentiaries and jails throughout the United States; Fraina, The Social Revolution in Germany; Marriage a Life-Long Honeymoon (anon.); Bernarr McFadden, Diseases of Men and Super Virility of Manhood; Horace W. C. Newte, The Lonely Lover; Mark Ryce, Mrs. Drummond's Vacation; Hubert Wales, Cynthia in the Wilderness; With Drops of Blood the History of the Industrial Workers of the World Has Been Written (anon. pamphlet).

36. Hansard, op. cit., April 7, 1927, p. 2031.

37. Ibid., April 7, 1927, p. 2035.

38. Ibid., April 14, 1927, p. 2506.

39. Ibid., April 1, 1927, p. 1775.

40. Ibid., April 7, 1927, p. 2035; July 17, 1931, p. 3887.

41. Ibid., July 17, 1931, p. 3887.

42. Ibid., June 1, 1931, p. 2172-73.

43. Ibid., July 17, 1931, p. 3878.

44. Ibid., June 1, 1931, p. 2175; July 17, 1931, pp. 3889-91; March 13, 1936, p. 1063; January 18, 1937, p. 32.

45. Ibid., July 17, 1931, pp. 3880-89.

46. Ibid., July 17, 1931, p. 3889.

47. Ibid., March 13, 1936, pp. 1062-69.

48. Who's Who in Canada, 1930-31.

49. Globe and Mail, June 2, 1931, p. 14.

50. Ibid.

51. Ibid., p. 1.

52. Ibid., June 5, p. 2.

53. Ibid., p. 2.

54. See Hansard, July 17, 1931, pp. 3892-93.
55. Ibid., March 13, 1936, pp. 1059, 1062-69.
56. Ibid., April 25, 1933, p. 4288.
57. See Hansard, February 25, 1936, pp. 490-517.
58. This view was expressed by a Liberal member, J. A.
Bradette. Hansard, March 5, 1936, pp. 789-90.
59. Hansard, February 7, 1938, p. 240.
60. Ibid., March 23, 1937, p. 2052.
61. Ibid., March 13, 1936, p. 1054-69.
62. Report of the Special Senate Committee on Mass
Media, 3 (Ottawa, 1970), 210. In 1939 Canadian Magazine
announced that it could no longer publish. For a good summary of the pre-Time-Reader's Digest era, see B. K. Sandwell, "The Magazine Problem," Saturday Night, April 8, 1939,
p. 9.
63. Hansard, June 13, 1940, p. 751.
64. W. Eggleston, "The Press of Canada," Royal Commission Studies (Arts, Letters and Sciences) (Ottawa: King's
Printer, 1951), p. 41.
65. Report of the Royal Commission on National Development in the Arts, Letters and Sciences (Ottawa: King's
Printer, 1951), p. xi.
66. Eggleston, op. cit., p. 52.
67. Royal Commission on National Development, op. cit.,
p. 64.
68. See article on Periodical Press Association submission to Massey Commission in Financial Post, November 26,
1949, p. 9, "Magazine Publishers of Canada Demand that They
Get 'Even Break in Own Land.'" See also B. K. Sandwell,
"Periodical Press and the Massey Report--Fourth Estate:
Power or Pressure," Saturday Night, August 28, 1951, p. 12.
69. R. L. Perry, "Here's Story behind New Magazine
Tax," Financial Post, March 31, 1956, p. 8.
70. Hansard, August 7, 1956, p. 7169.
71. Ibid.
72. Ibid.
73. Ibid.
74. Perry, op. cit., p. 8.
75. Hansard, March 20, 1956, p. 2333.
76. Ibid., March 20, 1956, pp. 2333-34.
77. Globe and Mail, March 21, 1956, pp. 1, 10.
78. Hansard, March 23, 1956, pp. 2552-76.
79. Ibid., March 27, 1956, p. 2669.
80. Ibid., March 27, 1956, p. 2670.
81. Ibid., March 23, 1956, pp. 2552, 2576. F. A.
Healy, general manager of the Association of Canadian Advertisers, sent a letter to the Finance Minister on April 3,

1956, strongly objecting to the 20 percent tax and stating
that such a tax would actually decrease the amount of advertising revenue available to Canadian magazines. Hansard,
August 7, 1956, p. 7174. This argument was reintroduced
by Canadian magazines in the hearings before the Senate
Committee on the Mass Media. (See Chapter 5.)

82. Hansard, March 28, 1956, p. 2696; August 7, 1956,
pp. 7171-72.

83. Ibid., April 9, 1956, p. 2737.

84. This argument was enunciated by Michael Starr,
the Conservative member from Ontario. Hansard, March 27,
1956, p. 2670.

85. Globe and Mail, March 21, 1956, p. 10.

86. Hansard, March 6, 1957, p. 1926; March 26, 1957,
p. 2684.

87. New York Times, March 23, 1956, 23: 3.

88. Ibid., April 23, 1957, 50: 4.

89. Globe and Mail, March 21, 1956, p. 10.

90. Ibid.

91. Hearings of the Royal Commission on Publications, 6
(Ottawa: Queen's Printer, 1961), 14.

92. Hansard, July 13, 1960, p. 6175.

93. "The Magazine Tax," Canadian Commentator, 3, no. 1
(January 1959), 4-7.

94. Hansard, September 3, 1958, p. 4559.

95. Ibid., July 28, 1960, p. 7178; August 6, 1960, pp.
7704-6.

96. Quoted in G. Dexter and J. A. Stevenson, "Canada's
Tariff Reprisals Against America," Current History, 34
(1931), 208.

97. H. G. J. Aitken, "Defensive Expansionism: The
State and Economic Growth in Canada," in Aitken, ed., The
State and Economic Growth (New York: Social Science Re-
search Council, 1959), pp. 79-114.

THE ROYAL COMMISSION ON PUBLICATIONS:
THE HEARINGS

The order-in-council justified the government's establishment of a Royal Commission on two counts: first, "that Canadian magazines and periodicals add to the richness and variety of Canadian life and are essential to the culture and unity of Canada," and second, "that it has been alleged that because of inequitable competition from foreign periodicals of various forms the publication of Canadian magazines has been prejudicially affected."[1]

Proceeding from this, the terms of reference for the commission were specified as follows:

(a) to inquire into and report upon the recent and present position of and prospects for Canadian magazines and other periodicals with special but not exclusive consideration being given to problems arising from competition with similar publications which are largely or entirely edited outside of Canada or are largely or entirely foreign in content; and

(b) to make recommendations to the Government as to possible measures which, while consistent with the maintenance of the freedom of the press, would contribute to the further development of a Canadian identity through a genuinely Canadian periodical press.[2]

Although we are emphasizing the issues related to consumer periodicals, it should be noted that the commission also considered business, trade, and farm periodicals and scholarly, cultural, and scientific magazines.[3]

Appointed as commissioners were M. Grattan O'Leary, president of the Ottawa *Journal* and a resident of Ottawa;* John George Johnston, chairman of the Toronto public relations firm of Johnston, Everson & Charlesworth Ltd.;** and Claude P. Beaubien, vice-president in charge of public relations and advertising of the Aluminum Company of Canada Ltd.*** The staff of the commission consisted of eight mem-

---

*M. Gratton O'Leary was born in 1889 and joined the Ottawa *Journal* in 1911. He was a member of the Ottawa Press Gallery from 1911 to 1925 and unsuccessfully ran for Parliament in the riding of Gaspé in 1925. He was a press correspondent at the 1921 Imperial Conference and at the Disarmament Conference in Washington in the same year. O'Leary was a delegate to the Imperial Press Conference in Australia in 1925, one of a group of Canadian journalists invited by the British government to report on Britain's war effort in 1941, and a press correspondent at the Potsdam Conference in Berlin in 1945. He became president of the Ottawa *Journal* in 1957, and at the time of his appointment to the commission he was president, publisher, and chief stockholder of the *Journal*. O'Leary was summoned to the Senate on September 24, 1962. He retired from journalism in 1963 but retained his presidency of the *Journal* until 1966, after which he became editor emeritus. In 1967 he became one of the "Ten Famous" Canadian journalists since Confederation placed in the Newspaper Hall of Fame in the Parliament buildings.[4]

**John George Johnston was born in Hillburgh, Ontario, in 1895 and joined the Buffalo *Courier* in New York State as a reporter in 1916. From 1916 to 1926 he occupied the position of editorial writer with the *Express* in Buffalo, New York. From 1926 to 1931 he worked for the *Financial Post* in Toronto, and from 1931 to 1964 he was with Johnston, Everson & Charlesworth Ltd., Toronto, finally as chairman of the board. This firm edited and published the "Printed Word" from 1931 on. In 1964 he became proprietor of the J. G. Johnston Association, writers on public relations.[5]

***Claude P. Beaubien was born in 1908 and joined the Aluminum Company of Canada Ltd. in 1936. He was appointed personnel director at Shawinigan works in 1939, moved to Arvida in 1942, was appointed Quebec City sales manager in 1947, and then was transferred to Montreal in 1949. At the time of his appointment to the commission, Beaubien was vice-president in the public relations and advertising branch of Alcan.[6]

bers; the interests of central Canada (Ontario and Quebec) were heavily represented and constituted a potential bias that caused concern to other interests in eastern and western Canada and in the United States.

The commission was authorized to investigate every aspect of the Canadian periodical industry and not just the results of foreign competition. Yet there could be no doubt that American magazines, particularly those with special Canadian editions, were the focus of the inquiry. The issues had been narrowed down to two critical contentions, (1) that the unrestricted incursion of foreign periodicals attenuated Canadian culture and unity and (2) that alien magazines enjoyed competitive advantages not shared by the native industry. There was no mention made of the threat to other Canadian manufacturers posed by foreign advertisements or the morally debilitating effects of salacious literature. What was implied was an economic and cultural analysis of the magazine industry.

Nine months elapsed between the appointment of the commission on September 16, 1960, and the time the report was tabled in the House on June 15, 1961. Thirty-one days, between November 14, 1960, and January 20, 1961, were devoted to hearings and the personal presentation of submissions. Tables 3.1 and 3.2 show the distribution of the participants in the commission's hearings by region, city, and type.

A detailed list of all the participants included in Table 3.2 appears in Appendix A. It should be noted that the figure "141" participants represents a total of the numbers of distinct participants making representations in each of the various cities, although some of them appeared in more than one city and therefore figure more than once in this total.

In all, about 130 separate interests* appeared before the Royal Commission, while an additional 35 simply submitted briefs (2 in Vancouver and 33 in Ottawa). Interests such as Time, Reader's Digest, Maclean-Hunter, and the Periodical Press Association made representations and pleaded their causes on numerous occasions. At the close of the hearings, 188 briefs had accumulated for the commission's consideration.[7]

The data in Tables 3.1 and 3.2 reveal that the commission concentrated its inquiry in Ontario and Quebec, espe-

---

*This number will vary depending on how the interests are separated; it should not be considered an exact figure.

TABLE 3.1

Royal Commission on Publications,
Hearings by Region and City

Region and City	Number of Days of Hearings	Total Days of Hearings per Region	
		Number	Percent
Central Canada		25	81
Ottawa	14		
Toronto	5		
Montreal	5		
Quebec	1		
Western Canada		5	16
Vancouver	3		
Regina	1		
Winnipeg	1		
Eastern Canada		1	3
Halifax	1		
Total		31	100

Source: Compiled by the authors from data contained
in Appendix A.

cially in the cities of Ottawa, Toronto, and Montreal; the
geographic location of most of the Canadian publishing business dictated this, since interests such as Maclean-Hunter
and Reader's Digest, along with influential manufacturing
groups, were situated in these places. There was nothing
intrinsically undesirable in this situation except that the
interests of central Canada might not coincide with the
interests of the remaining regions in Canada, especially
when the imposition of a tariff was at stake. Eastern and
western Canada appeared to be allocated a peripheral role
in the inquiry, with the prospect that their views would
influence the outcome of the investigation less, which could
drastically affect their interests. No hearings were held
in four of the provinces: Alberta, New Brunswick, Newfound-
land, and Prince Edward Island.

The East and the West actually found potent allies in
Time and Reader's Digest, strange as these bedfellows might

TABLE 3.2

Number of Participants in Royal Commission on Publications,
Hearings by Region, City, and Type

Region and City	Number of Participants by Type					Number of Participants by City	Total of Participants by Region	
	Canadian Publishers	Foreign Publishers	Publishers' Associations	Business	Other		Number	Percent
Central Canada	25	12	16	17	38		108	78
Ottawa	6	7	8	3	14	38		
Toronto	11	4	5	4	11	35		
Montreal	6	1	3	10	11	31		
Quebec	2	––	––	––	2	4		
Western Canada	7	1	4	––	14		26	17
Vancouver	4	1	2	––	10	17		
Regina	––	––	––	––	1	1		
Winnipeg	3	––	2	––	3	8		
Eastern Canada	3	––	––	1	3		7	5
Halifax	3	––	––	1	3	7		
Total	35	13	20	18	55		141	100

Source: Compiled by the author from data contained in Appendix A.

44

TABLE 3.3

Participants in Royal Commission on Publications
by Type and Region

	Region	
Type	Central Canada	Eastern and Western Canada
Publishing interests	53	15
Business interests	17	1
Other interests	38	17

Source: Compiled by the authors from data contained in Appendix A.

appear to be; the demands of these areas had more in common with those of the foreign interests than they had with central Canadian demands. Tables 3.1 and 3.2, of course, bury the actual economic and political influence of the participants, particularly Time and Reader's Digest, which were able to bring to bear pressures from the U.S. government.

ANALYSIS OF SUBMISSIONS

From the 130 publishing, business, government, individual, and other assorted interests that reported to the O'Leary commission, we have selected the submissions of 39 parties in order to make a detailed analysis of their views and recommendations. The sample was chosen after all the submissions had been examined.

It was soon noted that there were areas of concern common to certain groups, based largely on their geographic location. On the basis of this we decided to examine selected submissions in depth. These submissions are identified below. This sample may be broken down into three loose clusters of interests: (1) "national" concerns located in central Canada (Ontario and Quebec); (2) those regionally based participants situated in eastern and western Canada; and (3) foreign (U.S.) and internationally oriented publishing interests. In the central Canadian group the Periodical Press Association and the Maclean-Hunter organization shared the limelight, while Time and Reader's Digest

were by far the leading defenders of American investment
and interests. Eastern and western Canada appeared to have
no guiding, significant voices; there were only isolated
and rather inconsequential cries, of negligible impact.
We will examine the positions of the three groups with regard to their views on the economic state of the Canadian
periodical industry and the cultural identity problems resulting from the dominance of foreign literature, and their
attitudes toward protectionism as it relates to the publishing industry. Attention will also be drawn to the position
of the ethnic press and the French-language press.

Central Canada
(Ontario and Quebec)

The 20 submissions studied in this group include:

The Association of Canadian Advertisers, Inc.
The Canadian Association of Advertising Agencies
Canadian Labour Congress
The Canadian Manufacturers Association
Canadian Pulp and Paper Co., Ltd.
Department of Public Printing and Stationery
Maclean-Hunter Publishing Co.
The Magazine Publishers Association
McClelland and Stewart Ltd.
Monetary Times Publications Ltd.
Mutual Standard Publishing Co.
National Business Publications Ltd.
The Periodical Press Association
Simpson-Sears Ltd.
Southam-Maclean Publications
T. Eaton Company Ltd.
Toronto Star Ltd.
Toronto Telegram
University of Toronto Press
Wallace Publishing Co.

A kind of "collective will" emerges from this group,
in that their views, either tacitly or explicitly expressed,
display an extremely high degree of homogeneity. A strong
consensus of opinion about the cultural significance of
Canadian magazines and the economic predicament of the industry was revealed, although the precise nature of the desired government remedial action sparked some discord. Following is a synopsis of the views and recommendations of

this central Canadian group, dealing with the three areas
of interest noted above. Emphasis will be laid on the views
articulated by the Periodical Press Association and Maclean-
Hunter.

It was alleged that Canadian magazines were not in a
healthy, flourishing, and developing state, as shown by
their dismal financial record, and that future prospects
were discouraging.[8] In a word, their very survival was at
stake. This contention echoes back to the very birth of
the Canadian magazine industry, which had never really got-
ten from the fledgling state to a point of takeoff. It was
conceded that better management along with improved editorial content were desired in some instances, but that
these were minor problems compared with American overflow
circulation, split runs, regional editions, and special Canadian editions. Advertising revenue is the very lifeblood
of the magazine industry; it was argued that Time and Reader's Digest, by their unfair competitive advantages, were
able to reap a disproportionate share and thereby seriously
detract from the success of Canadian publications. This
situation had been going on since 1943 and had reached an
intolerable point by the mid-1950s.

By 1960 there remained only eight Canadian general
circulation magazines of substantial circulation: Canadian
Homes, Chatelaine, Chatelaine-La Revue Moderne, Liberty,
Maclean's, La Revue Populaire, Le Samedi, and Saturday Night.
Maclean-Hunter, the lucrative business publications of
which subsidized its general circulation magazines, feared
further losses of native financial resources through the
entrance of foreign publishers into the field of business
papers.[9]

In sum, the central Canadian position stressed that
the economic environment was extremely hazardous and inequitable, mainly because of U.S. competition. Time
and Reader's Digest, specifically, were the home industry
with backbreaking financial difficulties. If jungle law
continued to govern the periodical industry, it was contended
that Canada would soon be left with only a handful of regional publications.

The central Canadian group tediously reiterated that
magazines were a chief encouragement of national identity
and awareness.[10] It was argued that such a function was
solely a prerogative of nationals: aliens, insensitive to
the nuances of Canadian life, were incapable of truly interpreting Canada's national experience and of awakening
the nation's consciousness. This group asserted that Canada's cultural distinctiveness was gravely impaired by the

onslaught of American literature, which served not only to obscure Canadian culture but to instill foreign values in the Canadian psyche. The impression given was that without Canadian magazines there would be no Canadian culture and that Canada would eventually be absorbed by the United States. The publishing interests of central Canada probably belabored this point unnecessarily, for by that time the cultural significance of indigenous periodicals had been recognized in the 1951 Massey Report and the Liberals' 1956 tax amendment, verbally extolled by all political parties, and emphasized in the orders-in-council establishing the Royal Commission.

Protection is very much a part of the economic makeup of central Canada. The periodical industry had agitated for protection from time to time, with the government assisting it for two brief periods numbering six years in all from 1931 to 1936 and from 1956 to 1957. During the hearings the Periodical Press Association cogently requested tariff protection and proposed several forms that such a tax might assume.[11] In the 1920s and 1930s central Canadian manufacturers had had much to gain from restraints on the entry of American magazines with their advertisements, but after the war the complexion of industry changed as more American subsidiary firms entered Canada and the nationality of the advertisers took on less significance. In general, however, protectionist sentiment predominated within the central Canadian group.

The extent to which the cultural cry simply concealed a desire for commercial protection is difficult to ascertain. Any government assistance would first have had to buttress the financial position of Canadian publishers if it were to have any long-run effect on culture; this ultimately reduces the cultural problem to one of economics. Any industry that is operated for a dual purpose, to make money and to enhance culture, is always suspect when it seeks assistance. During the hearings Canadian publishers stressed the cultural motive, although subsequent events shed some doubt on their credibility in this.

The Maritimes and the West

The 12 submissions studied in this group include:

The Atlantic Advocate
The Dartmouth Free Press
The Halifax Board of Trade

48

Government of Saskatchewan
Mrs. Pat Hanley for Pirate Magazines
Stuart Keate for the Victoria. Daily Times
Major-Way Press Ltd.
Public Press Ltd.
Mrs. C. L. Shaw for Construction World and Mil-
    ler Freeman Publications
Stovel-Advocate Publications Ltd.
Winnipeg Master Printers and Lithographers As-
    sociation

In general, the Maritime Provinces and western Canada
differ from central Canada in that they are less indus-
trialized, have a lower per capita income, display a greater
sense of regionalism, and are ethnically more heterogeneous.
These differences naturally give rise to differences of interest, especially in matters affecting the tariff. Publishing concerns in these areas concentrate on reflecting
local and regional life and make little attempt to present
a national perspective. These areas appeared to have little say in the commission's investigation, with their publishing interests granted a total of only six days of hearings. This detachment regarding the proceedings of the inquiry was brought out by the then premier of Nova Scotia,
R. L. Stanfield, in his welcoming words to the commissioners
in Halifax.

> You may find . . . and I am not sure . . . that
> perhaps there will not be so many appear before
> you from our Province as has been the case in
> certain other Provinces. . . . We have here in
> this region some distinguished publications, but
> it may be they are not in such keen competition
> with foreign journals. . . . For this reason per-
> haps this topic is not of such exciting interest
> here as it is in some other parts of the country,
> because it may be that the periodicals that are
> most in danger are some thousand miles from
> here.[12]

In general, these submissions reveal a striking com-
placency about the economic health of Canadian periodicals.
The small, regional publications of most direct concern to
them were surviving: this was taken as tangible evidence
that the industry was not all that badly off. The natural
hazards of publishing in a country like Canada were often
cited as major impediments to successful magazine publish-

ing, but there was a noticeable tendency to blame the Canadian publishers, who were alleged to be reluctant to invest in risky ventures and who were often managerially incompetent. _Time_ and _Reader's Digest_ were exonerated, to some extent, from the accusation of unfair competition leveled on them by Ontario and Quebec publishers. The publications in these areas did not experience the full impact of foreign competition and were largely immune to the effects of _Time_ and _Reader's Digest_ on the amount of available advertising revenue because of the local nature of their publishing enterprises. This aloofness from the front lines in central Canada, where the real battle was waged, left these regions with a sense of security about the publishing business as a whole.

The bond between national magazines and national awareness was not always intuitively recognized in these areas, and the prosperity of central Canadian publishing houses was not necessarily equated with the cultural vitality of Canada. Culture was not a major topic of discussion in the briefs submitted by the publishing interests in these regions; but then, these interests had less reason to extol the cultural virtues of Canadian magazines because they had less at stake in the outcome of the commission. If central Canadian publishers seemed to show too much concern for national culture, perhaps the publishing interests of eastern and western Canada displayed too little, describing _Time_ and _Reader's Digest_ not as insidious instruments of American imperialism emasculating Canadian culture but as valuable cultural attributes interpreting Canada to a widespread audience.

Protection has unpleasant connotations in the Maritimes and western Canada. It has always been felt that tariffs assisted business in Ontario and Quebec at the expense of the outlying regions of Canada. R. Morton, publisher of _The Dartmouth Free Press_, expressed this view as follows:

> We feel that as one of the less economically prosperous provinces of the Dominion we have suffered from it [the tariff] in undue proportion, but protection we have and on protection central Canada has prospered.[13]

In the past, the tariff has meant higher consumer costs with little offsetting benefits to industry in these regions. Protection for Canadian periodicals was viewed as just another installment in the overall protectionist framework. Once again, as happens every time government action to assist the publishing industry comes under discussion, the principle of press freedom was invoked incessantly. Not all publishing concerns in these regions greeted the prospect of tariff protection with outright abomination,* but, on the whole, there was little enthusiasm displayed for the protective measures demanded by central Canada, especially in the Maritime Provinces, which opposed the tariff almost unanimously.

The United States

The seven submissions studied in this group include the following:

The Hearst Corporation
Macfadden Publications Inc.
The McCall Corporation
The McGraw-Hill Publishing Co.
Newsweek, Inc.
The Reader's Digest Association (Canada) Ltd.
Time International of Canada Ltd.

Only two members of this group, _Time_ and _Reader's Digest_, are of significant interest, for only these two produced special Canadian editions designed to attract a substantial slice of the advertising revenue. Although the circulation of the remaining American publications was high in Canada, they solicited either a negligible amount of Canadian advertisers' dollars or none at all. The problem of foreign periodicals should have been quite simple, since it was reduced to only two publications, but these magazines had two rather decisive characteristics working in their favor: first, they happened to be _Time_ and _Reader's Digest_, which together wielded an extremely formidable amount of political and corporate influence; and second, they happened to be owned in the United States. Any attempt by Canada to upset their Canadian operations might have had economic and political repercussions in other areas.

Over the years, the exact health of Canadian periodicals has been hard to define. At almost any point in its

---

*Mrs. Pat Hanley of Pirate Magazines, Mitchell Press Ltd., Public Press Ltd., Stovel-Advocate, and the Winnipeg Master Printers and Lithographers Association supported tariff protection.

rocky history this industry could accurately be described
as swaying on the brink of extinction; yet Canadian magazines have continued to exist. Time, for its own reasons,
described the industry as a fine example of Canadian commercial initiative at its very best, and concluded that

> the Canadian magazine industry in its entirety
> is flourishing and expanding at a rapid rate
> . . . and that the competition from foreign
> periodicals, whether equitable or inequitable,
> has negligible effect on the health and sta-
> bility of the magazine industry in Canada.[14]

There could be little doubt that as far as Time and Reader's
Digest were concerned, business was in fact booming. The
Canadian publishers who criticized American magazines for
exercising "unfair" competitive advantages pointed out that
these U.S. subsidiaries enjoyed access to the vast resources
of their parent firms and simply packaged editorial material prepared in America under the guise of a Canadian product. In reply these "maple leaf" editions of U.S. periodicals argued that editorial content was only a small consideration in the overall financial operations of a publishing
company and did not constitute an inequitable advantage.
Furthermore, Time and Reader's Digest argued that they enhanced the magazine field as a medium for advertisers to
the great advantage of the entire industry. In the unset-
tled state of the Canadian periodical industry at this
time, the validity of this argument was just beginning to
be realized.

   Time and Reader's Digest did not perceive themselves
as exacerbating the cultural identity problem in Canada,
but on the contrary portrayed themselves as important vehicles contributing to the development and definition of Canadian culture. Each went to elaborate lengths to document
its involvement in the Canadian community and the amount
of Canadian content contained on its pages. This led L. E.
Laybourne, managing director of Time (Canada), to assert
that "so much Canadian news is carried in Time that it may
be said confidently that no other journal provides as much
information about Canada to as many readers throughout the
world."[15] Ironically, this statement came appallingly close
to the truth. These magazines described themselves as an
integral part of the solution, rather than a thorny part
of the problem, of Canada's identity crisis.

   Culture had not been a major concern in the periodical
debate initially, but by 1960 it was being emphasized in-

creasingly. In this context it was imperative that _Time_
and _Reader's Digest_ dwell on their cultural contribution
to Canada, since the fate of their Canadian operations depended partly on convincing the commissioners that they
performed a desirable cultural function.

Tariff protection would not necessarily affect all
foreign publications. The 1931 tax had affected only magazines with specific amounts of advertising, while the 1956
tax affected all special editions of American magazines,
independent of the amount or nationality of their advertisements. The Canadian publishers were out to protect Canadian advertising revenue from the grasp of foreign publishers; if protection had been complete, _Time_ and _Reader's
Digest_ would probably have been forced to suspend their
Canadian operations. Therefore the American publishers
joined with the Maritime and western Canadian group in pro-
testing against any contemplated infringement of press freedom. Both groups abhorred the thought of a protected Canadian publishing industry, but for obviously different reasons.

Summary of Views Expressed
by English-Language Publishers

The views elaborated on in the preceding section are
summarized in Table 3.4.

On a continuum, the views expressed by central Canada
and the United States would represent the polar extremes,
while eastern and western Canada would occupy the middle
ground, but inclined toward the American views. Some of
these views are irreconcilable; someone had to get hurt by
whatever position the Royal Commission adopted. The Maritimes and western Canada, which in a number of ways represented a compromise position, were not leading actors in
the commission's proceedings: the publications battle narrowed down to two extreme groups, with the Periodical Press
Association and Maclean-Hunter representing the Canadian
position and _Time_ and _Reader's Digest_ representing the
American interest.

The Views of the French
and Ethnic Presses

So far we have ignored the views expressed by non-
English publications. Both the French-Canadian and the

TABLE 3.4

Summary of Views Expressed by Interest Groups
Divided Geographically

Subject Matter of Views	Opinions of Interest Groups by Region		
	Central Canada	Maritimes and West	United States
Economic health of Canadian magazines	Desperate	Perhaps less healthy than desirable	Prosperous
Concern for Canadian culture	Great concern	Mild concern	Sensitive
Desire for protection	Impose tariff	No tariff	No tariff

Source: Compiled by the authors.

ethnic presses presented submissions to the commission,
and their views provided further input into the commission's
deliberations. However, in their cases, the language barrier partially shielded them from concern with foreign periodicals.

The overall health of Quebec magazines was not so
vigorous as one might have expected. By 1960 there were
only three periodicals of general interest: La Revue Populaire and Le Samedi, which were both published by Poirier,
Bessette et Compaigne, Ltée; and La Revue Moderne, which
was taken over by Maclean-Hunter in 1960.

Imported magazines from France were found in abundance
on Quebec newsstands. This was the French-language equiva-
lent of the competition from U.S. overflow circulation experienced by the English-language magazines. Respecting
these periodicals from France, the report states:

The imported magazines have the advantage of
editorial content underwritten by a large domestic market. And this editorial material is of a
level which cannot be afforded or matched by the
French-Canadian publisher.[16]

54

However, the real threat to the French-Canadian publishers came from Reader's Digest, which published a French
edition, and Maclean-Hunter, which offered Chatelaine-La
Revue Moderne and Le Magazine Maclean. These publishers were
able to offer special low combined rates to advertisers
who opted to place advertisements in both editions. Quebec
publishers were unable to make such attractive offers because they had no English-language editions, and therefore
they complained that they were forced to compete on inequitable terms with magazines of far greater resources than
they had.[17]

The ethnic mix in Canada is partially nourished by a
polyglot press, which publishes in more than 25 languages.
The copious influx of new Canadians since World War II has
greatly increased the number of ethnic papers, which provide a profusion of cultural stimuli and facilitate a blend-
ing of the old with the new. Unlike the English-language
publications, these ethnic papers are generally immunized
to U.S. competition because of the language barrier, although most Jewish papers, such as the Canadian Jewish
Chronicle of Montreal and the Icelandic Chronicle of Winnipeg, publish in English. Furthermore, these papers, the
majority of which are published by ethnic organizations,
are not national competitors seeking to reach all segments
of society; rather their appeal is to relatively small and
sometimes diverse, ethnically distinct groups.

The commission received representations from the
Canada Ethnic Press Federation (CEPF), the Canada Press Club
of Winnipeg, the Canadian Ethnic Press Club of Toronto, and
National Publishers Ltd., but in its report the subject of
the ethnic press was dismissed in six sentences.

The CEPF brief to the commission listed its four major
purposes as follows:

1. To study and interpret the Canadian scene and the
integration of ethnic cultures into that scene, and thus
to contribute to a more united and richer Canadianism.
2. To promote a better understanding and cooperation
among the various ethnic groups in Canada.
3. To study and interpret Canada's role in international affairs and her position among the nations that up-
hold the ideals of freedom and democracy.
4. To gather and disseminate information that will
lead to a better appreciation of the basic principles to
which Canada is dedicated, and provide a forum for the study
and discussion of problems common to Canada's ethnic press
and to foster its welfare.[18] These objectives suggest that

the function of the ethnic press is largely educational; it introduces the Canadian way of life to newcomers while maintaining linkages with societies left behind. This role placed the ethnic press outside the battle being waged by national publishers against certain foreign publications.

NOTES

1. Report of the Royal Commission on Publications (Ottawa: Queen's Printer, 1961), p. 107.
2. Ibid.
3. Royal Commission, op. cit., Chaps. 6, 7.
4. The Canadian Parliamentary Guide, 1971; The Canadian Who's Who, 1968.
5. Who's Who in Canada, 1968; The Canadian Who's Who, 1968.
6. The Canadian Who's Who, 1968.
7. This number is cited by the commission. Royal Commission, op. cit., p. v.
8. Periodical Press Association submission to Hearings of the Royal Commission on Publications, 1 (Ottawa: Queen's Printer, 1961), 31; vol. 31, pp. 12-32; Maclean-Hunter submission, vol. 2, p. 6; vol. 30, pp. 164-70.
9. Maclean-Hunter submission, Hearings, vol. 2, p. 15; These losses are substantiated in the report of the financial consultant to the commission, Royal Commission, op. cit., pp. 160-61.
10. Periodical Press Association submission, Hearings, vol. 1, p. 31; Maclean-Hunter brief, vol. 2, pp. 18, 90.
11. Periodical Press Association brief, Hearings, vol. 31, pp. 39-56. Maclean-Hunter brief, vol. 31, pp. 63-68.
12. Hearings, November 30, 1960, Halifax, vol. 12, p. 6.
13. Hearings, vol. 12, p. 82.
14. Hearings, vol. 3, p. 7.
15. Hearings, vol. 3, p. 19.
16. Royal Commission, p. 44.
17. Poirier, Bessette et Compaigne, Ltée. brief, vol. 24, pp. 2-13.
18. Hearings, vol. 10, pp. 10-11.

4

THE ROYAL COMMISSION ON PUBLICATIONS:
THE REPORT AND THE REACTION

THE REPORT

The commissioners prefaced their report with the statement:

> Only a truly Canadian printing press, one with
> the "feel" of Canada and directly responsible
> to Canada, can give us the critical analysis,
> the informed discourse and dialogue which are
> indispensable in a sovereign society.[1]

From this declaration of the cultural significance of
a native press, the commission reasoned that the government
has the responsibility to ensure that such periodicals are
not driven to extinction through unfair and foreign competition. The commission did not pretend that periodicals
are absolutely essential for the cultural vitality of a nation; rather it viewed them simply as a very significant
means of fostering Canadian identity.[2]

The health of the industry was assessed by examining
the number of births, deaths, and mergers of periodicals;
the distribution of advertising revenue; and the circulation
figures.[3] After applying these statistical yardsticks to
the Canadian magazine scene, the commission concluded that
the industry appeared to be in poor health in the sense
that, in the decade prior to the Royal Commission, there
had been a net reduction in the number of periodicals cir-
culating in Canada. (See Table 4.1.) At the same time,
Time and Reader's Digest had made the sharpest gains in
advertising revenue between 1950 and 1958, relative to the
gains made by all Canadian magazines. (See Table 4.2.)

TABLE 4.1

Births and Deaths of Magazines in Canada, 1920-60

Decade	Number Started	Number Discontinued or Absorbed
1920-29	96	23
1930-39	72	65
1940-49	87	70
1950-59	30	50
1960-69	250	137

Sources: Royal Commission on Publications (Ottawa: Queen's Printer, 1961), p. 14; Report of the Special Senate Committee on the Mass Media, 1 (Ottawa: Queen's Printer, 1970), 156.

The circulation of magazines in Canada by nationality of ownership, as published by the Audit Bureau of Circulations (A.B.C.) is shown in Figure 4.1, revealing that the share of total Canadian circulation of the Canadian A.B.C. magazines had fallen from 30 percent of the total in 1950 to 20 percent in 1959. In addition, a report by the financial consultant retained by the commission concluded that "Canadian consumer magazines are not in a healthy condition, as compared with either the 'Canadian editions' of Reader's Digest and Time, or U.S. magazine publishers."[4]

The economic issue concerned the problems of overflow circulation and byproduct circulation of foreign periodicals. In the case of overflow circulation, the foreign periodical circulated in Canada is identical to the periodical circulated in the country of origin. Advertising revenue lost to Canadian media results from the fact that U.S. parent companies with subsidiaries in Canada may not permit the subsidiaries to buy advertising in Canadian periodicals because the Canadian audience can be reached through advertising in U.S. periodicals that sell (overflow) in Canada.[5] This problem was compounded by the fact that two U.S. companies, Curtis Publishing Company and Select Magazines, a consortium of five U.S. magazine publishers including the publishers of Time and Reader's Digest, controlled about 40 percent of the distribution of magazines sold on newsstands in Canada.[6] By the copy, revenue is much higher from newsstand sales than from subscription sales because of the

cost of soliciting subscriptions; Canadian magazines obtained about 10 to 25 percent of their sales through newsstands, compared to 50 percent for U.S. magazines sold in
Canada.[7] The commission deemed overflow circulation to be
unfair competition for Canadian periodicals.

Byproduct circulation has several variants, including
split runs, regional editions, Canadian sections, and Canadian editions.[8] The feature of these variants that dis-
tinguishes them from overflow circulation is that the copies
sold in Canada differ in part, by way of advertisements
and/or editorial content, from those sold abroad, as a special attempt to tailor the periodical for the Canadian market. In the case of the Canadian edition, which includes
those of Time and Reader's Digest,

> A substantial amount of editorial material used
> in the parent edition is re-used in the "Canadian"
> edition. It is this re-use which gives the pub-
> lisher a decided cost advantage, because the
> profit on the sale of advertising space is greater
> when editorial material can be used again, in-
> stead of purchased anew.[9]

TABLE 4.2

Advertising Revenues of Magazines in Canada,
1950 and 1958

Recipients of Advertising Revenue	Amount Spent in 1950 (in dollars)	Amount Spent in 1958 (in dollars)	Percent of Increase
All of the media, including radio and television	233,997,000*	503,891,000*	115.3
All Canadian maga- zines	10,874,000	21,366,000	96.5
Leading Canadian consumer magazines	7,089,000	11,150,000	57.3
Time	1,177,000	3,622,000	207.7
Reader's Digest	1,558,000	4,582,000	194.1

*Estimated.

Source: Royal Commission on Publications (Ottawa:
Queen's Printer, 1961), p. 15.

The extra cost of using editorial material in an additional periodical is zero. The commission found that the total cost of the editorial material in Canadian editions was very low and that this constituted "dumping" of editorial material in Canada, which is a form of unfair competition to Canadian periodicals. No attempt was made to determine what a fair price would have been; it was merely noted that the Canadian editions of Time and Reader's Digest spend a much lower percentage of their revenue for editorial purposes than do Canadian periodicals.[10]

While overflow and byproduct circulation of French magazines did present some problems to French-Canadian periodicals, it was found that there was less incentive for French magazines to behave in this way because "there is, between France and French-Canada, little of the business integration that exists between the United States and Canada."[11] Even the ethnic press complained of some problems of byproduct circulation associated with European editorial material,[12] but the problems of the French and ethnic presses were largely ignored by the commission.

Overflow circulation appeared to be an unavoidable consequence of sharing a continent with the American giant, but special Canadian editions were viewed as posing a different and far worse problem on which the government could act. Since top-quality editorial material was "dumped" into Canada and packaged inexpensively as the Canadian editions of Time and Reader's Digest, and since the high quality and other resources at the command of these magazines were able to attract a large readership audience and greater than 40 percent of all the advertising revenue available to Canadian magazines,[13] to the minds of the commissioners this was unfair competition.

Following this analysis, the report concluded that "a nation's domestic advertising expenditures should be devoted to the support of its own media of communications"[14] and that "a genuinely Canadian periodical press can only exist by assuring for Canadian publications, under equitable conditions, a fair share of domestic advertising."[15] To this end the commission offered 13 recommendations, the two main ones being as follows:

(a) That the deduction from income by a taxpayer of expenditures incurred for advertising directed at the Canadian market in a foreign periodical, wherever printed, be disallowed, and

(b)   That the entry into Canada from abroad of a
periodical containing Canadian domestic advertising be excluded under Schedule C of
the Customs Act.[16]

If implemented, these recommendations would provide a
fair degree of protection for Canadian magazines. The cost
of Canadian advertising in foreign publications would be
approximately doubled, thereby, in all likelihood, squeezing
Time and Reader's Digest out of Canada.[17]   Hopefully, between 8 and 9 million dollars would be released from advertising in these magazines and redistributed among the remaining purely Canadian periodicals.[18]   The report offered
no corrective steps to curb overflow circulation, but
viewed this situation as an irremediable fact of life in the
Canadian publishing world. Obviously, the interests of
central Canada won out; they and the commissioners were
virtually of the same mind. This should not be interpreted
to mean that the inquiry was a conspiracy undertaken simply
to lend an element of legitimacy to the suppression of foreign interests by Ontario and Quebec publishers. It cannot
be determined to what extent central Canadian bias clouded
the investigation, but the Royal Commission appears to

FIGURE 4.1

Yearly Circulation in Canada of Canadian A.B.C.[a]
Magazines, Reader's Digest, Time, and
U.S. A.B.C. Magazines, 1940-59

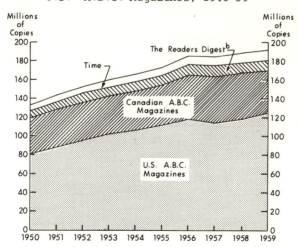

[a]A.B.C. = Audit Bureau of Circulation
[b]Includes English and French Editions

Source: Royal Commission on Publications (Ottawa:
Queen's Printer, 1961), p. 15.

have been persuaded by the logic of the situation presented
by these interests. In short, Canadian publishers had a
strong case, and this is reflected in the commission's analysis and recommendations.

A Royal Commission is only one step in the process of
policy formation and is a far cry from actual legislative
implementation. Central Canadian interests had won only a
battle, not the war, and the next round would see the
U.S. government intervene on behalf of Time and Reader's
Digest.

THE REACTION TO THE REPORT

As might be expected, the reaction of the press and
the various publishing interests to the report took on a
geographical flavor similar to the distribution of views
found in the submissions. C. V. Laurin, president of the
Periodical Press Association, appeared jubilant and felt
that the chances were "very good" that the government would
act on the O'Leary recommendations.[19] If carried out, they
would strengthen the entire publishing industry, make new
magazines possible, and give added incentive to Canadian
magazines already in the field. Numerous new jobs would be
provided for printers, writers, artists, and photographers.
F. S. Chalmers, president of Maclean-Hunter, stated that
the recommendations would create in Canada not only a
commercial climate conducive to the survival of existing
national magazines but also one favoring entrepreneurship
in the publications field.[20] Jack Kent Cooke, owner of
Liberty and Saturday Night, vividly asserted that the pa-
tient would not only recover but "should enjoy a healthy,
lusty and successful future" if O'Leary's proposals were
implemented.[21] Cooke was also joined by his editor, Arnold
Edinborough of Saturday Night, in praising and urging the
implementation of the report.[22] David Maclellan, general
manager of the Graphic Arts Industries Association, was
"delighted," and hoped that Parliament would give its unanimous approval to the report.

There will be far-reaching benefits in terms of
employment of Canadian printing craftsmen, artists, designers, writers, editors, salesmen and
clerical help, as well as increasing public
revenue and decreasing of pressures which have
raised the cost to Canadians of using their own
postal services.[23]

J. S. Atkinson, president of Toronto Star Ltd., welcomed the report with equal enthusiasm.[24] The report also received editorial support from the Montreal _Star_, the Montreal _Gazette_, the Ottawa _Citizen_, and the Windsor _Star_.[25]

One newspaper, the Toronto _Globe and Mail_,[26] which printed its weekend supplement in Buffalo,[27] criticized the report as an assault upon the basic principle of freedom of the press. Adding support to the _Globe_'s protest was Warren Reynolds, president of the Canadian Association of Advertising Agencies, who expressed deep concern over the proposal to disallow tax deductions on domestic advertising placed in foreign magazines.[28]

In the Maritimes, M. Wardell, publisher of the _Atlantic Advocate_ and the Fredericton _Gleaner_, termed the proposals both "wicked and foolish" because they demonstrated

a desire to discriminate against American-owned magazines that have been established in Canada in good faith with investments of millions of dollars and because it advocates what amounts to "sharp practice" by the Canadian government.[29]

Wardell found the report to be

incredible were it not for the hostility and bias against the so-called American publications demonstrated by the members of the commission during their hearings.[30]

In British Columbia Stuart Keate, publisher of the Victoria _Times_, stated:

I have always felt Canadian magazines, like any other Canadian business, should stand on their own feet or go under. Any way you slice it, the publications report is another example of Tory protectionism.[31]

In addition, the report was editorially attacked by the Fredericton _Gleaner_, the Halifax _Chronicle_, the Winnipeg _Free Press_, and the Vancouver _Province_.[32]

Representing American magazines, Lawrence E. Laybourne, managing editor of Time International of Canada, bluntly stated that the intent of the report was none other than to destroy _Time_'s Canadian operations.[33] In the period from the establishment of the commission in 1960 to the publication of the report in 1961, _Time_ made reference to the com-

mission in seven issues of its Canadian edition. Besides
reporting on the progress of the commission, Time implied
that the concern for Canadian culture was a pretended concern,[34] and that the commission was being used as a means
of getting protection for Canadian periodical interests,
especially Maclean-Hunter.[35] Another story refers to a
case of alleged anti-Semitism on the part of one of the
commissioners, J. G. Johnston.[36] References are made to
Canadians who are critical of the commission and its findings[37] and to the possibility that advertisers might divert
their business to other media if it was no longer attractive
for Canadians to advertise in foreign-owned periodicals.[38]
In general, Time used its Canadian edition to try to mold
opinion in its favor.

Speaking for Reader's Digest, President E. Paul Zimmerman found the report highly discriminatory against what he
considered to be a Canadian operation, even though Reader's
Digest claimed at no time to be a Canadian publication.
Time was ambivalent on this score. Some officials of Time
claimed it was a Canadian magazine, while the owner, Henry
Luce, stated, "I do not consider Time a Canadian magazine."[39]
The U.S. State Department withheld comment on the report
pending further consideration of the recommendations and
talks with the Canadian government. However, it was suggested that implementation of the recommendations would
conflict with the General Agreement on Tariffs and Trade
(GATT) to which Canada was a signatory.[40]

THE AFTERMATH OF THE REPORT

The commission report, which marked a high point in
the periodical debate, tendered a set of highly controver-
sial recommendations for final decision by political lead-
ers in Canada. The commissioners did not attempt to achieve
a compromise but firmly upheld Canada's cultural integrity
and called for legislative action that would in effect force
Time and Reader's Digest to pack up and leave. It was
highly unlikely that any government would adopt the drastic
proposals contained in the report as it was presented at
that time. Following the tabling of the report, the contend-
ing publishers regrouped and focused their arguments on the
Prime Minister and his cabinet and the members of the House.
Understandably, the government appeared reluctant to act
quickly and awaited the reaction of publishers and foreign
governments to the report in the hope that some less drastic
proposals might emerge. However, the various publishers

concerned failed to strike a truce, and Prime Minister
Diefenbaker found himself in the difficult position of having to decide the fate of the report and perhaps the fate
of Canada's few remaining magazines.

The story of the cabinet infighting that must have
followed the report has not been made public, but seven
months elapsed before the Conservative government was prepared to indicate its policy with regard to the publications
issue. On January 18, 1962, the Throne Speech forecasted
such government action:

> My government plans to recommend to you a number
> of measures that will constitute further steps in
> working out the purposes of confederation and
> identifying more clearly the Canadian nationality
> in various aspects of public and business affairs.
> With this purpose in mind, you will be asked to
> give effect, with modifications, to the recommen-
> dations of the royal commission on publications.[41]

Any modification in favor of _Time_ and _Reader's Digest_
would suggest that the views of the United States, which
were officially received by the Canadian government in
August of 1961, were not completely disregarded by Diefenbaker.[42] Surprisingly, the House did not have to wait long:
only four days after the Throne Speech, Diefenbaker suddenly
announced the government's intention to employ tariff regulations and tax penalties to curb the loss of Canadian advertising to American magazines.[43] The government intended
to implement the report's proposal that periodicals containing advertising primarily directed to the Canadian market
be denied entry to Canada from abroad. Also, the Royal
Commission's other major recommendation, which would prohibit deductions from taxable income for advertising directed to the Canadian market in a foreign periodical,
wherever printed, would be applied. However, this second
general rule was modified to the extent that expenditures
incurred for advertising directed to the Canadian market in
a foreign periodical already established in Canada (that
is, _Time_ and _Reader's Digest_), would be deductible to the
extent of only 50 percent. This proposed legislation would
go a great deal further to protect Canadian magazines than
any previous government had dared to suggest. By way of
justification for such a proposal Diefenbaker stated:

> We believe that this legislation is necessary in
> the interest of the Canadian identity and as an

assurance that Canada's destiny will be preserved.
. . . We in Canada believe we have the right to
assert the preservation of those things which are
Canada's and that our Canadian publishing industry is challenged in such a way that unless action
is taken we shall, in the days ahead, be dependent entirely or almost entirely on the viewpoint of another nation, however friendly.[44]

The report recognized that the recommendations might
involve GATT; the possibility was discussed at length by
the commission, and experts were consulted.[45] As was usual
in this investigation, opinions were divided. Nevertheless,
the commission decided to proceed with its proposals and
turn the problem over to the politicians. The U.S. government had been in touch with the Canadian government shortly
after the report was made public, and the economic implications of its proposals were informally discussed early in
January 1962 at an Ottawa meeting of the joint U.S.-Canadian
ministerial committee on trade.[46] The Conservative government was mindful of its international obligations and expressed its desire to hold consultations with any government
concerned, but Diefenbaker made clear that he did not view
the problem strictly as a commercial question within the
terms of GATT.

The Government has considered the relationship
between the recommendations of the royal commission and our commercial obligations to other
countries under the general agreement on tariffs
and trade. The commission establishes very
clearly that the issues at stake . . . are not
essentially of a commercial character but go
into the fabric of our culture.[47]

However, by these efforts to curb _Time_ and _Reader's
Digest_, Diefenbaker had incurred the wrath of the United
States, even though the proposed measures would not render
the Canadian operations of these companies impotent. There
remained a number of options open to foreign magazines
that would have countered the loss of income tax deductibility for their advertisers. First, if they simply left
their advertising rates unchanged, the ultimate cost including taxes to the advertiser would have been substantially
more than before; however, if Canadian advertisers considered _Time_ and _Reader's Digest_ the best buy, then the intent
of the legislation could have backfired, and Canadian pub-

lishers would have lost even more revenues. A second alternative would be to cut advertising rates to give advertisers the same space for the same money even with the loss
of tax deductibility. If these magazines could absorb the
financial loss then Canadian publishers would probably have
experienced very little gain. To assist Canadian publishers effectively, then, the government measures would have
had to be fatal to Time and Reader's Digest. A more last-
ing consequence of the intended legislation would be the
prevention of any other foreign publishers from duplicating
the success of these two magazines in Canada.

Predictably, the proposed legislation was warmly received by Canadian publishers. The Periodical Press Association's president, C. J. Laurin, stated, "This sets the
climate for Canadian publications that is required to produce a flourishing industry over many years."[48] F. S.
Chalmers, president of Maclean-Hunter, labeled the proposals
as "a very bold step that took a great deal of courage. . . .
Up to now starting a magazine in Canada was a sure way to
bankruptcy. Now we have a reasonable chance of success."[49]
Arnold Edinborough, publisher of Saturday Night and Liberty,
commented:

> This doesn't answer all our problems. It was more
> than I ever expected, and I am very happy. But
> we still have our own way to make. Time and
> Reader's Digest aren't going to give up without
> a struggle and other magazines will be entering
> the field. This removes the inequitable compe-
> tition and makes it possible for us to have a
> fair go.[50]

Warren Reynolds, president of the Canadian Association of
Advertising Agencies, viewed the proposed measures as

> fair and just to Canadian publishers. . . . It
> should give heart to Canadian magazines but they
> must produce a product that is wanted by the pub-
> lic. . . . I think probably Canadian magazines
> have better times ahead than ever but they'll
> have to make it on their own ability.[51]

In western Canada Stuart Keate, publisher of the Victoria
Times, was "disappointed. . . . I hope when the Conservatives are defeated that the Liberals will then throw out
this legislation."[52]

Reader's Digest was outraged and pleaded to present
its case directly before the Canadian Parliament. In a
prepared statement following Diefenbaker's announcement of
the proposals, E. P. Zimmerman, president of Reader's Digest,
had this to say:

> Our Canadian-manned and managed business is pro-
> viding employment for over 1,000 Canadians. . . .
> We will have to evaluate our position in light
> of the potential effects on our business and de-
> cide whether we can survive economically if Par-
> liament enacts the proposal put forward by the
> Prime Minister. . . . In the meantime, in view
> of the welfare of the many Canadians whose live-
> lihoods depend upon us and our record, we would
> hope that an opportunity will be provided for us
> to state our case before Parliament in advance
> of any parliamentary decision.[53]

Time, not having invested in Canada to the same degree as
Reader's Digest, remained reticent about the proposals.
The U.S. State Department was, however, deeply concerned.

> While we are sympathetic with the Canadian Gov-
> ernment's desire to foster the development of a
> publishing industry reflecting Canadian cultural
> aims, we think that the reportedly proposed tax-
> ation of this type is neither the proper nor
> practical method to reach this end. . . . We ex-
> pect to consider seeking an early opportunity
> to present our views to the Canadian Government
> on its proposed actions.[54]

Then, abandoning exhortation and laying bare the commercial
facts of the issue, the State Department official indicated
that the United States would seek some form of trade com-
pensation if the Canadian government followed through its
plans.

> We have stated the previous Canadian action was
> a breach of Canada's obligations under (GATT).
> We still contend this is so. . . . During con-
> sultations we would examine the proposals on
> the question of whether there would be arbi-
> trary damage and loss of U.S. trade in Canada.[55]

The proposals were held in abeyance for the remainder of the session, which terminated with the calling of a general election for June 18, 1962. Prime Minister Diefenbaker returned to office as head of a minority government and repeated his pledge to assist periodicals in the Throne Speech on September 27, 1962. "You will be requested to enact measures to give effect, with modifications, to certain of the recommendations of the royal commission on publications."[56]

At this time the Canadian political climate was quite unstable, and one suspects that the various domestic and foreign interests concerned refrained from overreacting to any Conservative proposals in anticipation of the Tory defeat that came the following year.

Following the federal election of April 8, 1963, the magazine problem was flung back into the lap of the Liberals. Their victory had to be encouraging to foreign interests, with the Conservatives removed from power and replaced by a political team noted for its more continentalist persuasion. The Throne Speech on May 16, 1963, outlining the Liberals' legislative program, was mute on the subject of publications, but the Throne Speech on February 18, 1964, gave notice to the House that "you will be asked to consider measures to strengthen the position of periodicals published in Canada."[57] There appear to have been two reasons behind this delay. First, Lester Pearson's cabinet, along with the Liberal caucus, was obviously divided on the issue; secondly, the government wanted time to consider the desirability of broadening the basis of its action to include foreign control of Canadian newspapers and possibly foreign control of TV and radio.[58]

Finally, on February 20, 1964, the Prime Minister observed that the economic position of Canadian magazines had continued to deteriorate because of the general climate of uncertainty, which had disrupted its advertising programs. To set the industry straight, Pearson proposed two measures.[59] First, the Income Tax Act would be amended to prohibit a taxpayer from deducting from his income, for tax purposes, expenditures after December 31, 1964, for advertising specifically directed at the Canadian market in non-Canadian periodicals. However, non-Canadian periodicals were not to include any special Canadian editions of foreign magazines already in existence, thereby exempting _Time_ and _Reader's Digest_. The second proposal was that Schedule C of the

Customs Tariff be amended to prevent the entry into Canada of split runs or regional editions containing advertising specifically directed at the Canadian market, and of magazines, including trade papers, if greater than 5 percent of their advertising content was directed at Canadians.

These proposals were a victory for _Time_ and _Reader's Digest_ and a turnaround from the Liberals' 1957 tax legislation. They built a protective wall around the only two magazines that Canadian publishers really viewed with concern, while excluding any new foreign competitors. From the standpoint of Canadian publishers this was, in effect, locking the fox in with the chickens.

Canadian publishers, while displaying mixed reactions, were clearly disappointed over Pearson's proposals because of the extreme leniency lavished upon _Time_ and _Reader's Digest_. C. L. Laurin, vice-president of the magazine division of Maclean-Hunter, termed the proposals "the best practical solution,"[60] and F. G. Brander, president of the Magazine Publishers' Association, found them "greatly encouraging. . . . Early implementation of the proposals means the Canadian magazine industry will develop a more favourable climate. I'm optimistic about the future."[61] D. Maclellan, general manager of the Graphic Arts Industries Association, was "very happy about anything that strengthens the periodical press."[62] J. A. Daly, president of Southam Business Publications Ltd., described the proposed legislation as "locking the door after the horse was stolen. . . . I can't see that this legislation is going to help Canadian magazines."[63] The Toronto _Star_ editorialized:

> This is a fatal weakening of the O'Leary Report.
> It will do absolutely nothing to help national
> magazines . . . in their struggle for survival.
> . . . Its announcement may well be the death-
> knell for Canadian national magazines.[69]

We can only guess why there was not more opposition from Canadian publishers to the legislation. These publishers probably recognized that the Liberals' 1965 proposal was the best deal they were likely to get. The industry, no doubt, was anxious to normalize its operations, and the new legislation at least promised some semblance of stability. The industry as a whole had suffered financially because of the uncertainty that shrouded the status of _Time_ and _Reader's Digest_ in Canada. Consequently, by this time part of the Canadian industry was less certain about the harmful effects of _Time_ and _Reader's Digest_ on native publications, and so refrained from raising a storm of protest.

Consensus within the Liberal party was not easily achieved, and another 14 months elapsed before the Minister of Finance, Walter Gordon, presented the relevant legislation in his budget speech on April 26, 1965.[65] The speech dealt with magazines and with the necessity of preserving Canadian ownership and control of newspapers, and outlined Pearson's previous proposals in proper legislative form.* The Income Tax Act would be amended as formerly indicated and would become effective January 1, 1966. _Time_ and _Reader's Digest_ were exempted by limiting the definition of a "non-Canadian" periodical to exclude magazines that "throughout the period of 12 months ending April 26, 1965 . . . were being edited in whole or in part in Canada and printed and published in Canada." (See Appendix D.) Both magazines were printed and published in Canada. _Reader's Digest_ had had an editorial office in Montreal since 1948, and _Time_ had opened one in Montreal in 1962; legislatively defined, _Time_ and _Reader's Digest_ were as Canadian as the maple leaf and beaver.**

Gordon also proposed an amendment to the Customs Tariff Act that simply repeated Pearson's words on the matter. Also of significance was reference by Gordon to the subsidized postal rates enjoyed by _Time_ and _Reader's Digest_.[66] It was mentioned that this imbalance was being studied as part of a general review of all postal rates and that the resulting legislation would eliminate the discriminatory subsidy reaped by certain "foreign" magazines.

In principle, this Liberal legislation was a repetition of the Conservatives' 1962 proposals. During the debate on the resolution to amend the Income Tax Act, Gordon, noting this rare case of admitted agreement, stated: "This Government, after giving the matter further consideration, decided that the measure proposed by our predecessors was a sound one."[67]

Both parties were painfully aware of the difficulties involved in attempting to legislate retroactively, as evidenced by the exemptions to be accorded _Time_ and _Reader's Digest_. Such exemptions were realized to be not in the best interest of Canadian magazines, and it was apparent that Gordon did not consider the legislation satisfactory. "I

---

*The proposed resolution brought down later, however, was presented in the Prime Minister's name and not Finance Minister Gordon's.

**Two small foreign-owned newspapers, along with two foreign medical trade magazines, were also exempted.

do not believe there is any solution to this problem which will please everybody. However, to do nothing . . . would be the worst course of all."[68] Thus, Gordon, a well-known nationalist, was pressured into supporting a policy alien to his political and economic outlook. Later, in commenting on this tax policy, Gordon writes:

> The matter came up when the automobile agreement was under heavy attack in Congress. Approval of the agreement might have been jeopardized if a serious dispute with Washington had arisen over Time. In the circumstances, I believe the decision to grant the exemption was realistic. Nevertheless, steering this part of the legislation through the House of Commons, and explaining the reason for the exemption to the Liberal Party caucus, was one of the most unpalatable jobs I had to do during my period in government.[69]

An observation by R. W. Prittie, of the New Democratic Party, augments this point:

> From all his [W. Gordon's] past statements it is much contrary to the thinking of the Minister of Finance--One can only conclude that the pressure in the Cabinet was such that the Minister of Finance had to bow to the wishes of someone and is loyally going along with the decision which has been made.[70]

The familiar and pat criticisms were resurrected once again in objection to the Liberal legislation. The tax was pointed to, almost perfunctorily, as an oppressive limitation of press freedom, and it was suggested that restrictive measures were no guarantee that Canadian magazines would actually gain in advertising revenue.[71] But what really aroused the opposition's ire was the exemption of the very magazines most destructive to the Canadian publications industry.[72]

The bill was also criticized because of the omnibus nature of the amendment, which coupled two themes: section 12A(2) dealt with the tax treatment of advertising in magazines, while section 12A(4) covered the same issue, but with different treatment, for newspapers.[73] The second section was acceptable to many to whom the first was not, but the Liberals insisted on presenting this package as an all or nothing deal. Until 1965 there was no law discouraging for-

eigners from buying out Canadian newspapers. A few newspapers in eastern Canada apparently pressed for legislation
that would ensure the preservation of Canadian ownership
and control of Canadian newspapers, probably fearful that
when a newspaper came up for sale they would be unable to
meet the offers made by foreign newspapers. Gordon, in
his Budget Speech, said, "Given the vital role newspapers
play in influencing public opinion, we do not believe we
should run the risk of them falling under foreign control."[74]
The Income Tax Act was to be so amended that advertisements
placed in foreign newspapers and directed at the Canadian
public were not deductible for income tax purposes. The
preventive legislation would effectively remove any incentive for foreigners to buy Canadian newspapers.[75]

There appeared to be a real contradiction in principle
couched in the bill: Canadian newspapers were protected
from foreign ownership and control while, in the same
breath, Time and Reader's Digest were granted honorary Canadian citizenship. Further, this bill defined these magazines
as Canadian; yet the government indicated that they would
be considered as foreign with reference to the subsidization
of postal rates. An amendment proposed by Douglas Fisher
of the New Democratic Party that would delete section 12A(2)
was frustrated on procedural grounds, while a similar motion by Stanley Knowles of the New Democratic Party failed
to carry.[76]

Time and Reader's Digest, which had been under heavy
attack since the early 1950s, finally had their status in
Canada legally stipulated by Gordon's tax amendment. The
Canadian publications industry would simply have to adjust
to their government-sanctioned presence. To Gratton O'Leary
the measures were nothing short of "fraud" in claiming to
assist Canadian periodicals.[77]

Apparently the United States was not appeased by the
Liberal concessions, however, for both Undersecretary of
State George Ball and former Secretary of the Treasury Douglas Dillon still intimated that the United States would consider economic retaliation.[78]

PRESSURE-GROUP ACTIVITIES

A tracing of the pressure-group activities indulged in
by the major actors involved in the magazine issue provides
a broader understanding of the events and factors that shaped
the 1965 legislation. The Maclean-Hunter organization, along
with its mouthpiece, the Periodical Press Association, which

had previously spearheaded the efforts of central Canadian publishers, gradually faded from view shortly after the Royal Commission Report. Douglas Fisher suggests that Maclean-Hunter, along with Saturday Night, resigned itself to the American assessment of the problem.[79] E. P. Zimmerman of Reader's Digest convincingly argued that the best thing for publishers to do was to get together and reach some accord, and thereby achieve some stability in the magazine field. This would be followed by a concerted effort at organizing a magazine bureau that would attempt to popularize advertising in magazines and hopefully wrest back advertising revenue from the broadcasting medium. In other words, firms in the periodical industry switched from fighting each other to combining with each other to fight the other media for advertising revenue.

At this time Maclean-Hunter became fearful that McGraw-Hill, the most powerful of the U.S. trade publishers, was about to invade Canada. Rumors had it that McGraw-Hill had leased some property in the Toronto area and was definitely intending to enter the field of Canadian business publications.[80] This naturally struck terror at Maclean-Hunter, the business papers of which brought in its greatest profits. It therefore seemed worthwhile to refrain from opposition to Time and Reader's Digest in exchange for Gordon's legislation blocking the threat of trade publications. Under these conditions Maclean-Hunter accepted Zimmerman's business logic, and all mention of Canadian culture was sidelined.

With the surrender of Maclean-Hunter, the influence of central Canadian publishers was somewhat deflated; yet in the campaign to purge the industry of Time and Reader's Digest the banner continued to be carried by the Montreal Star, the Toronto Star Weekly and the Toronto Star, the Family Herald Weekly Star, and Weekend Magazine.[81] Of all the Canadian magazines, Weekend Magazine was in the best financial health, which enabled it to avoid the accusation of seeking to advance its own self-interest, although in the end these magazines were the losers.

The American publishers employed some persuasive tactics in Canada that were probably more appropriate in the context of their own political system.* Shortly after Dief-

---

*Also, following the Royal Commission Report, Reader's Digest had made representations to various employee associations and cabinet ministers threatening the layoff of 400 Digest employees if the proposals were implemented.[82]

enbaker announced his intention to implement the Royal Commission's major recommendations in modified form, Reader's Digest went over the heads of the politicians and appealed directly to its Canadian readership "to interest [itself] in this sore problem."[83] Zimmerman's "Open Letter" described Reader's Digest's "cruel dilemma" and stressed the unfairness of the proposals and the likely economic loss to Canada if the Digest had to pull out. (See Appendix D.)

Douglas Fisher found himself subjected to severe pressure from the Provincial Paper Mill in his constituency of Port Arthur, which depended on Time and Reader's Digest for a large proportion of its sales.[84] The management and workers there, including the unions, suddenly began to overwhelm Fisher with correspondence demanding that Time and Reader's Digest be left alone as Canadian magazines consuming Canadian paper. Fisher received encouragement from Canadian publishers, however, especially in a letter dated May 4, 1965, from Mark Farrell, managing editor of Weekend Magazine, which outlined the problems of the industry.[85]

Besides beseeching members of the House through leaflets and personal contacts, these two magazines made the most of their relationship with the Liberal party. John Turner, Liberal M.P. for St. Lawrence-St. George and Parliamentary Secretary to the Minister of Northern Affairs and National Resources, represented the constituency in which Time operated an editorial office, while Time's Canadian edition was printed in the town of Mount Royal, represented by Liberal Allan Macnaughton, Speaker of the House of Commons. Also, Reader's Digest was compiled in a leased building in the riding of St. Antoine-Westmount, represented by the Liberal Minister of Industry, C. M. Drury. Such crucial contacts in the higher echelons of decisionmaking provided these companies with very significant political leverage and ensured that the Liberal party would not be insensitive to their interests.[86]

The efforts by Time and Reader's Digest to protect their Canadian investment were supported by the concern expressed by the U.S. government, which cried breach of trade obligations and threatened economic retaliation from the beginning of this debate. David Maclellan, general manager of the Graphic Arts Industry Association, was greatly annoyed by the U.S. government's intervention in what appeared to be basically a domestic problem.

The unwarranted interference . . . in Canadian affairs connected with the work of the Royal Com-

mission on Publications comes with bad grace and
should stop at once. . . . From the very first
day of the hearings of the [Commission], the
weight and the presence of the State Department
have been felt, and felt too much. . . . We wish
their government would mind its own business
when Canadians are discussing domestic problems
created by the merchant publishers of the U.S.[87]

Immediately following the report of the Royal Commission, a senior White House representative reportedly warned
that implementation of the commission's proposals would result in the immediate cancellation of a major U.S. aircraft
components contract then under negotiation at Canadair Ltd.
in Montreal.[88] Recalling the magazine tax, Gordon later
commented on the manner in which

the U.S. State Department went into action. Its
representatives urged on behalf of the whole U.S.
administration that nothing should be done which
would in any way upset or annoy the late Mr.
Henry Luce, the proprietor of Time.
    It was submitted that Mr. Luce had great
power in the United States through his magazines,
Time, Life and Fortune, and that if he were irri-
tated, the results could be most damaging both to
Canada and the U.S. administration.*
    The Canadian government concluded, quite
rightly in my opinion, that there was considerable
validity to these assertions respecting the influence of Mr. Luce and, accordingly, the Canadian edition of Time magazine was exempted from
the proposed legislation.[91]

Canada's western oil production was highly dependent
on the U.S. market; Washington threatened to review Canada's
quotas on exports of oil to the United States unless the

---

*On June 21, 1961, six days after the Royal Commission
report was tabled, Diefenbaker informed the House that the
U.S. government had been in touch with his government on
June 14 about the report's major proposals and had requested
an opportunity for consultation.[89] He also stated that on
August 4, 1961, the U.S. ambassador in Ottawa had acquainted
the Canadian government with the U.S. views about the magazine issues.[90]

Canadian government yielded.[92] However, the real clincher
at the time appears to have been that the U.S.-Canada automotive agreement would have been placed in grave jeopardy
had Canada failed to submit to the State Department's requests.[93] In spite of the din the various Canadian publishers had created over the magazine issue, Washington, sensitive to Luce and Reader's Digest, quietly helped to sway
Canada's publications policy to the detriment of Canadian
publications.

TIME AND READER'S DIGEST, 1960-65

Between 1960 and 1965 the Canadian magazine industry
experienced a sharp drop in advertising revenue. Reader's
Digest's revenues fell by 35 percent.[94] A year or so after
the Income Tax Amendment, Canada's major periodicals acted
on Zimmerman's advice and set up an association, the Magazine Advertising Bureau, for promotional purposes. Banded
together in this clique were Time, both French and English
editions of Reader's Digest, the two editions of Maclean's,
the three editions of Chatelaine, Saturday Night, Actualité,
the United Church Observer, and TV Hebdo.[95] Such strange
bedfellows would have been impossible to envisage at the
time of the Royal Commission inquiry, when cultural considerations seemed paramount in the minds of Canadian publishers. However, it would be unfair to call such a step the
sellout of Canadian culture. The Canadian government had
refused to grant the magazine industry the protection it
demanded and instead gave Time and Reader's Digest a priv-
ileged status. Canadian publishers, abandoned to fend for
themselves, adjusted to the situation.

These tax concessions did not signal the end of government harassment of Time and Reader's Digest; rather, the
government shifted its attention to a less critical cause,
but one that aroused fairly intense feelings. Many resented
the fact that these magazines, along with Canadian magazines
mailed in Canada, paid only one-third of their total mailing
costs while Canadian taxpayers footed the bill for the remaining two-thirds.[96] For example, it was estimated that
prior to April 1, 1969, the subsidy to Time amounted to
$864,000 and to Reader's Digest, $982,000.[97] On October 31,
1968, an amendment to the Post Office Act took effect that
defined Time and Reader's Digest as non-Canadian periodicals,
thereby reducing their subsidies to $721,000 and $852,000,
respectively, while at the same time giving the Minister
discretionary powers to adjust postal rates for non-Canadian

periodicals. (See Appendix E.) Therefore, despite the amendment, _Time_ and _Reader's Digest_ still enjoyed a substantial subsidy, and this was criticized by some.

This criticism was part of a wider belief that Canada is on the losing end of the Universal Postal Convention, whereby governments are required to handle all mail that is passed on to them by foreign post offices free of charge.[98] This arrangement is reciprocal, but Canada loses in the sense that it receives far more second class mail from abroad, mainly from the United States, than it sends. It was estimated that out of a deficit of $22 million on second class mail operations, in 1960, about $6 million was attributable to U.S. publications mailed in the United States.[99]

The American publishers and government had a much more direct impact on Canadian government periodical policies between 1960 and 1965 than before that time. By the time the Income Tax Amendment had been introduced in 1965, it seemed that Maclean-Hunter, for one, had come to believe that harsh treatment of _Time_ and _Reader's Digest_ would not direct advertising revenues to its publication. This may have been because of the declining proportion of advertising revenues that was being attracted to magazines. (See Appendix C, Table C.1.) It is interesting to note that it was _Reader's Digest_, a U.S. firm, that was instrumental in establishing a trade association, the Magazine Advertising Bureau, for the Canadian periodical industry. This may reflect the fact that American businesses have had more experience in organizing industry lobbies.

NOTES

1. _Report of the Royal Commission on Publications_ (Ottawa: Queen's Printer, 1961), p. 2.
   2. Ibid., p. 93.
   3. Ibid., p. 14.
   4. Ibid., p. 175.
   5. Ibid., pp. 47, 192.
   6. Ibid., p. 33.
   7. Ibid., p. 34.
   8. For details, see Ibid., pp. 10-13.
   9. Ibid., p. 13
  10. Ibid., p. 40.
  11. Ibid., p. 44.
  12. Ibid., p. 45.
  13. Ibid., p. 16.
  14. Ibid., p. 76.

15. Ibid., p. 74.
16. Ibid.
17. Ibid., p. 78.
18. Ibid., p. 100.
19. Toronto _Star_, June 16, 1961, p. 51.
20. _Globe and Mail_, June 16, 1961, p. 22.
21. Ibid.
22. Ibid.
23. Ibid.
24. Ibid.
25. Ibid., June 19, 1961, p. 6.
26. Ibid., June 17, 1961, p. 6.
27. J. A. S. Evans, "The O'Leary Report," _The Canadian Forum_, August 1961, pp. 97-98. The Royal Commission report was also attacked by the Thomson newspapers, which printed their monthly supplement, _Ontario Today_, in the United States.
28. _Globe and Mail_, June 16, 1961, p. 22.
29. Ibid.
30. Ibid.
31. Toronto _Star_, op. cit., p. 51.
32. _Globe and Mail_, June 19, 1961, p. 6.
33. Ibid., June 16, 1961, p. 22.
34. _Time_ (Canada), December 26, 1960, pp. 42-43.
35. Ibid., June 23, 1961, pp. 5-6.
36. Ibid., January 20, 1961, p. 12.
37. Ibid., February 3, 1961, pp. 10-11; July 7, 1961, p. 7.
38. Ibid., June 23, 1961, pp. 5-6.
39. Royal Commission, op. cit., p. 97.
40. _Globe and Mail_, June 16, 1961, p. 22. For a brief survey of U.S. editorial reaction to the report see "U.S. Views Magazine Commission," _Financial Post_, July 15, 1961, p. 17.
41. _House of Commons Debates_, January 18, 1962, p. 2. [Hereafter referred to as _Hansard_.]
42. _Globe and Mail_, January 25, 1962, p. 19.
43. _Hansard_, January 22, 1962, p. 59.
44. Ibid., January 24, 1962, p. 141.
45. _Globe and Mail_, op. cit., p. 19.
46. Ibid.
47. _Hansard_, January 22, 1962, p. 60.
48. _Globe and Mail_, January 23, 1962, p. 8.
49. Toronto _Star_, January 23, 1962, p. 4.
50. _Globe and Mail_, op. cit., p. 8.
51. Toronto _Star_, op. cit., p. 4.
52. Ibid.

53. Ibid.
54. Globe and Mail, January 24, 1962, p. 1.
55. Ibid.
56. Hansard, September 26, 1962, p. 7.
57. Ibid., February 18, 1964, p. 2.
58. Ibid., December 21, 1963, p. 6282.
59. Ibid., February 20, 1964, pp. 57-58.
60. Toronto Star, February 21, 1964, p. 2.
61. Ibid.
62. Ibid.
63. Ibid., February 22, 1964, p. 4.
64. Ibid., February 24, 1964, p. 6.
65. Hansard, April 26, 1965, p. 435.
66. Ibid.
67. Ibid., June 14, 1965, p. 2385.
68. Ibid., June 22, 1965, p. 2787.
69. Walter Gordon, A Choice for Canada (Toronto: Mc-Clelland and Stewart Ltd., 1968), p. 97.
70. Hansard, June 16, 1965, p. 2509.
71. Ibid., June 15, 1965, pp. 2422-27, 2438; June 16, 1965, pp. 2504-2511.
72. Ibid., June 22, 1965, pp. 2795-98.
73. Ibid., pp. 2796-97. For details of the amendment see Hansard, June 14, 1965, p. 2382.
74. Hansard, April 26, 1965, p. 435.
75. Globe and Mail, April 27, 1965, B-6; Winnipeg Free Press, April 27, 1965, p. 9.
76. Hansard, June 15, 1965, pp. 2466-69; June 28, 1965, p. 2878.
77. Toronto Star, April 27, 1965, p. 1.
78. Ibid., p. 9.
79. Hansard, June 15, 1965, p. 2435.
80. Ibid.
81. Ibid., June 15, 1965, pp. 2434-35.
82. Hansard, June 28, 1960, p. 7184.
83. Reader's Digest, March 1962. (See Appendix D.)
84. Hansard, June 15, 1965, pp. 2435-36.
85. Ibid., p. 2466.
86. Guy Marcoux cited an article in the Montreal Star dated March 19, 1964, that alluded to this point. Hansard, March 20, 1964, pp. 1313-1314; see also Douglas Fisher, Hansard, June 15, 1965, p. 2435.
87. Globe and Mail, January 25, 1962, p. 19.
88. P. C. Newman, The Distemper of Our Times (Toronto: McClelland and Stewart Ltd., 1965), pp. 224-26.
89. Hansard, June 21, 1961, p. 6815.
90. Ibid., September 11, 1961, p. 8155.

91.   Speech in May 1969 by Gordon, cited in <u>Report of</u>
<u>the Special Senate Committee on Mass Media</u>, op. cit., vol.
3, p. 213.
92.   P. C. Newman, op. cit., pp. 224-26.
93.   Ibid. Also Gordon, op. cit., p. 97.   See also K.
Lefoli, "What the Tough Talk from the State Department
Means," <u>Maclean's</u>, June 6, 1964, pp. 1-2.
94.   <u>Report of the Special Senate Committee on Mass</u>
<u>Media</u>, op. cit., vol. 3, p. 213.   See also Table A.1.
95.   Ibid., p. 227.   For a description of the structure and purposes of the Magazine Advertising Bureau of
Canada, see the report prepared by the bureau for the Senate
Committee.   Also, <u>Proceedings of the Special Senate Commit-</u>
<u>tee on Mass Media</u>, no. 22 (Ottawa: Queen's Printer, Feb-
ruary 19, 1970).
96.   <u>Hansard</u>, October 24, 1968, p. 2057.
97.   Ibid., May 5, 1969, p. 8295.
98.   Ibid., May 19, 1966, p. 5335.
99.   Royal Commission, op. cit., p. 87.

5

THE SENATE COMMITTEE REPORT
ON THE MASS MEDIA

By 1968, for many, the publications issue was a dead horse not to be revived. The rules had been defined and the industry was adjusting accordingly. The Royal Commission Report had barely had time to gather dust, however, when the Canadian Senate initiated a second look at the economic health and future prospects of the native mass media, including magazines.

This study was the brainchild not of the publishers, but of Senator Keith Davey, a man not only intensely interested in the subject of mass media but also highly experienced in the field. Davey first gave notice of such a study on November 19, 1968,[1] and two months later, on February 4, 1969, moved

> that a Special Committee of the Senate be appointed to consider and report upon the ownership and control of the major means of mass public communication in Canada, and in particular, and without restricting the generality of the foregoing, to examine and report upon the extent and nature of their impact and influence on the Canadian public.[2]

What he proposed was essentially

> an objective, detached, dispassionate study of the relationship between these media and the people of Canada in order to determine the adequacy for Canada of its mass media in these changing times.[3]

Because the mass media include television, radio, newspapers, and periodicals, the study naturally encompassed many broad and diverse aspects, but its general concerns were the ownership, structure, and control of the media and their influence on the Canadian public. In discussing the major concerns of the study, Senator Davey underlined the fact that Canadian magazines still faced two special problems: (1) overflow of advertising and circulation from the United States and (2) uneven competition from special Canadian editions. Observing that 21 magazines* in Canada had suspended operations since the Royal Commission Report, Davey commented that "Senator O'Leary's predictions have certainly been borne out. . . . The situation is bad and getting worse."[6] However, magazines were only of interest to the senators insofar as they comprised one sector in the general field of mass communications. Senator Davey's motion met with no opposition and was passed on March 18, 1969. The committee was reconstituted by the Senate on October 29, 1969, and on October 8, 1970, and the final report was tabled in the Senate on December 9, 1970.

The committee was originally composed of the following 18 Senators:[7] L. P. Beaubien, K. Davey, P. Desruisseaux, D. D. Everett, L. Giguère, H. W. Hays, O. L. Irvine, J. K. Laird, J G. Langlois, J. M. Macdonald, C. R. McElman, W. J. Petten, J. H. Prowse, H. O. Sparrow, E. W. Urquhart, F. C. Welch, G. S. White, and H. A. Willis. By the time the committee reported, Desruisseaux, Giguère, Irvine, Laird, Langlois, Urquhart, White, and Willis had dropped out to be replaced by R. Bourque, M. E. Kinnear, J. D. Quart, D. Smith, and P. Yuzyk.

Chairman of the committee was Keith Davey, who had served his apprenticeship in the mass media field during his ten years of selling advertising for Toronto's CKFH radio. He had been sales manager of CKFH when Pearson appointed him executive director of the Liberal party, which position he had held from 1961 to 1966. Davey was appointed to the Senate by Prime Minister Pearson on February 24, 1966. In June, shortly after this appointment, he briefly served as commissioner of the Canadian Football League, but resigned in 1967.

---

*Senator Davey gave this figure but did not specify which or what type of periodicals they were.[4] In the Senate Committee report, however, it was noted that 250 magazines were begun in Canada and 137 died.[5]

Sitting as deputy chairman of the committee was Senator L. P. Beaubien, a millionaire Montreal industrialist who held directorships in Canadair, Empire Life Insurance Co., Dominion Structural Steel Ltd., London and Yorkshire (Canada) Ltd., and Beaubien Ltée.[8]

It is equally enlightening to focus on the extra-Senatorial support solicited by the committee. Davey turned to the men who knew the mass media best and hired several distinguished journalists. The study of press profits, the heart of the report, was directed by Bruce MacDonald, formerly a political and economic reporter for the Toronto Star and the Globe and Mail, and later an adviser to the federal Finance Department. The committee's executive consultant was Borden Spears, formerly an editor of the Toronto Star and Maclean's Magazine. Tom Sloan, previously a Quebec City correspondent for the Globe and Mail and the Montreal Star, and now senior assistant to R. L. Stanfield, leader of the opposition, researched the media of Quebec for the committee. The ghost writer behind the final report was Alexander Ross, on leave from the Financial Post.[9]

All of the Senate Committee's hearings were staged in Ottawa between December 9, 1969, and April 24, 1970. During these sessions more than 100 witnesses made personal presentations and the committee was deluged with about 500 briefs.[10] Table 5.1 is a breakdown of the number of mass media witnesses according to their types of media. A detailed list of these interests appears in Appendix B.

More French-Canadian interests participated in the Senate Committee's hearings than in the Royal Commission, but because of the scope of the inquiry this is probably true for Maritime and western Canadian interests also. Like the Royal Commission, which had heard only from Poirier, Bessette et Compaigne (publisher of La Revue Populaire and

TABLE 5.1

Media Interests by Type and Number

Type of Interest	Number Appearing
Periodical	24
Newspaper	42
Broadcasting	27
Other	20
Total	113

Le Samedi), and <u>Actualité</u>, the Senate was host to only a
few French periodical publishers, <u>Actualité</u>, Les Journaux
Trans-Canada Ltée., and Pierre Peladeau, president of
Quebecor Inc. The remaining French Canadians represented
newspaper interests; they kept to their own particular field
and did not usually comment on the magazine problem.

In spite of its mandate to review the publications issue, the Senate Committee hearings failed to engender the
heated debate among publishers that had so enlivened the
Royal Commission sittings. The situation had changed.
First of all, the magazine industry was legislatively
stable, and neither the publishers nor the government were
anxiously awaiting the outcome of the Senate's study. No
surprises were expected, and most publishers were probably
downright bored by the debate at this stage. Of greater
significance was the détente reached within the industry
through the alliance of <u>Time</u> and <u>Reader's Digest</u> with Canada's major publishers in the formation of the Magazine
Advertising Bureau. Since the presence of these foreign-
owned magazines was now felt to be best for business, it
was tacitly assumed that their presence was best for Canada
as well. The last moderating factor appears to have been
the relative insignificance of the Senate study, which al-
lotted only a minor portion of its time and effort to the
magazine problem. Undoubtedly, to many, the great publications debate was over before the Senate Committee began its
hearings.

ANALYSIS OF SUBMISSIONS

Only the submissions of the 24 periodical interests
plus a few others are pertinent to this study. Our original
intention was to employ the same format of analysis we used
in our study of the submissions to the Royal Commission.
Unfortunately, the virtual nonparticipation of magazine interests from eastern and western Canada prevented a grouping
of the periodical participants along the same regional lines
as presented previously; however, our sample of 17 selected
interests lends itself to division into central Canadian and
American groups. The views of these two groups will be outlined, with special emphasis on any change in their views
since the Royal Commission report. Note will also be taken
of the position of the French-Canadian and ethnic publishers.

Central Canada (Ontario and Quebec)

The 15 participants include the following:

Actualité*
The Canadian Business Press
The Canadian-Star Weekly*
The Chatelaine group (English and French editions)*
The International Typographical Union
Maclean-Hunter*
Maclean's*
Saturday Night
The Southam Business Press*
The Southam Press Ltd.
Southstar Publications Ltd.
Toronto Calendar Magazine
The Toronto Star*
The Toronto Telegram
Weekend-Perspectives*

In 1960 central Canadian publishers were almost completely unanimous in their condemnation of Time and Reader's
Digest as parasitic intruders contributing nothing to the
cause of Canadian identity. By 1970 these same publishers
were clearly divided on the issue. The non-establishment
sector of the industry--non-Magazine Advertising Bureau members such as The Canadian Business Press, The Canadian Star-
Weekly, The Southam Business Press, Southstar Publications
Ltd., the Toronto Star, and Weekend-Perspectives--still
perceived their self-interest, and Canada's, to be directly
at odds with Time and Reader's Digest and urged the implementation of the Royal Commission's proposals. Their general position has been outlined previously and there is
little need for repetition here.

What is of special interest is the turnaround in the
position of Canada's major publishers with regard to the
desirability of Time and Reader's Digest in Canada. All
Canadian members of the Magazine Advertising Bureau--the
two editions of Maclean's, the three editions of Chatelaine,
Saturday Night, Actualité, the United Church Observer, and
TV Hebdo--vigorously defended the status quo and stressed
the benefits accruing to the industry by virtue of the co-
operative presence of Time and Reader's Digest. R. A.

---

*These interests took part in the Royal Commission
hearings.

McEachern of Maclean-Hunter pointed out that without _Time_
or _Reader's Digest_ in Canada there would be fewer magazines
among which the creative and production costs of advertising
could be distributed, thus making the medium as a whole a
less attractive buy.[11] The best-reasoned defense of _Time_
and _Reader's Digest_ was articulated by _Toronto Calendar
Magazine_, which also recommended that _TV Guide_ be awarded
exemption status.[12]

Toronto Calendar argued that the presence of _Time_ and
Reader's Digest enhanced the health of the magazine industry and that the removal of their special status would prove
harmful to all concerned. Further, the removal of their
tax exemption would effectively raise their advertising
rates by 50 percent, with the magazines and their advertisers
absorbing this increase; these Canadian advertising dollars
would not be directed to other Canadian magazines. In addition, it was argued that if _Time_ and _Reader's Digest_ left
Canada it would hurt Canadian-owned advertisers without
harming the advertising of U.S. subsidiaries, which benefit
from their parents' advertising in U.S. magazines. The
U.S. subsidiaries (the majority of _Time_ advertisers) would
not substantially increase their advertising budgets for
other Canadian magazines. The ousting of _Time_ and the _Di-
gest_ would thus gravely reduce the economy of advertising
campaigns and therefore depreciate the value of magazine
advertising for agencies and clients. Newspapers and supplements would gain by such a change, but not other magazines.

Corporation executives, on occasion, display schizoid
characters. Casting off their corporate mask, some leading
editors unveiled their personal feelings in letters that
much impressed Senator Davey. P. C. Newman stated:

> As the new editor of _Maclean's_, highly conscious
> of the fact that every word and every photograph
> and illustration that goes into the magazine is
> originated and paid for in this country, I find
> it incomprehensible that two American magazines
> should be allowed, with government sanction, to
> pass off what are almost entirely American pub-
> lications . . . as Canadian magazines, attracting
> Canadian advertising.
>
>   Since the local editors of _Time_ and the _Di-
> gest_ are directly responsible to their American
> head offices where the final decisions about
> what goes into their magazines are made, they do
> not and in fact, cannot accurately reflect the

Canadian reality in the very few pages they rele-
gate to Canadian news. Only truly Canadian magazines can fulfill this essential mandate.

[Maclean's will be able to achieve its as-
pirations] only if Time and Reader's Digest revert to what they really are: American magazines
which should be coming into this country on
exactly the same basis as all other U.S. publications.[13]

This is a concise restatement of Maclean-Hunter's position
during the Royal Commission inquiry. Doris A. Anderson,
editor of Chatelaine, wrote,

few people would suggest today that it was a good
idea to allow the Canadian editions of Time and
Reader's Digest to compete in Canada for advertising on equal terms with completely Canadian
periodicals. . . . [Their] continued presence is
crippling for the Canadian magazine industry . . .
the situation will almost certainly deteriorate.
. . . I think if we care about Canada and a strong
periodical press (and I don't think the two can
very well be separated) then action to end the
special Canadian editions of Time and Reader's
Digest must be taken.[14]

Highlighting the Senate Committee hearings was the ap-
pearance of Senator Gratton O'Leary who appeared disillu-
sioned by the events subsequent to his report. He observed
that Canadian magazines were less Canadian in 1970 than in
1960 and that they were not trying hard enough to interpret
Canadian life. Senator O'Leary no longer felt that Canadian
magazines were worth protecting, since they were not even
trying to help themselves but instead sanctioned, through
partnership, the presence of Time and Reader's Digest. He
stated: "I have no praise for existing Canadian magazines."[15]

In sum, one group of Canadian publishers sustained
the assault against Time and Reader's Digest in the interests of the native industry and Canadian cultural development, while the establishment sector of the industry not
only supported the status quo but also maintained that the
two foreign-owned magazines were essential to the economic
vitality of the industry.

The United States

Only two publications represented American interests--
Time and *Reader's Digest*. Both magazines no longer felt
threatened, and consequently their whole posture was more
relaxed and coolheaded.[16] Essentially their position was
the same as it had been in 1960, but their defense of it
was less feverish. Both magazines still maintained that
their Canadian presence did not impose unfair competition
on the Canadian magazine industry, which *Time* assessed as
"not in an unhealthy position." Neither publication attempted to document its contribution to the development of
Canadian artistic talent and culture in the thorough way it
had for the Royal Commission. Indeed, there was no need
to do so. The industry was widely divided on the issue.
It was highly unlikely that the Canadian government, for
fear of U.S. economic retaliation, would enact restrictive
measures, and Canada's leading publishers were defending
their presence. Their initiative in forming the Magazine
Advertising Bureau had paid handsome dividends in the form
of allies in the magazine industry.

The French and Ethnic Presses

The problems of the French-language press and publications were neglected by the Senate inquiry, as they had
been by the Royal Commission. No substantive mention is
made of French-language magazines in the chapter of the
Senate's report entitled "The Troubled Magazines."[17]
The ethnic press, however, did receive greater attention from the Senate Committee, which provided a forum for
the Canada Ethnic Press Federation, *Canadian Scene*, and
Corriere Canadese, and cast its analytic net somewhat further
than the Royal Commission, allotting five pages to the subject of ethnic publications.[18]
The Canadian Ethnic Press Federation (CEPF) submission
to the Davey Committee summed up the function of the ethnic
press as follows:

> To those people who, at one time or another,
> have shown themselves behind the language barrier
> in a country whose laws, traditions and customs
> were different from their own, the Ethnic Press

has been a guide, an interpreter, a teacher and an intimate friend; its role has been to introduce an immigrant into his new environment as efficiently and as painlessly for himself and for the community, as possible.[19]

The CEPF also perceived itself as somewhat of an ideological crusader. In its brief to the Senate Committee the Federation stated:

The Ethnic Press has also helped to introduce newcomers who had not been exposed to the benefits of the democratic institutions, to the new way of life and to shield others from adverse influence or ideological currents opposed to democracy in Canadian tradition.[20]

The CEPF viewed Canada's bilingual nature as a potentially invulnerable bulwark against U.S. cultural domination and felt that this would remain so as long as the two dominant groups interacted harmoniously.[21] Ethnic groups, argued the CEPF, act as a buffer by preventing the polarization of the two major national forces and thereby contribute to Canadian identity and unity. Naturally, the role of the ethnic press in ensuring the vitality of these groups was stressed.

In sum, the ethnic press played the part of a didactic big brother in easing the integration (not assimilation) of newcomers into Canadian society and in encouraging the preservation of the cultural and linguistic heritage of the various ethnic groupings.

In its various briefs, the ethnic press cited the following difficulties as being of most immediate concern. First, rising costs, which have afflicted the publishing industry as a whole, are especially troublesome for the poorly financed ethnic press. The 1969 increase in postal rates probably struck a harder blow to the ethnic press than to any other sector of the publishing industry. The CEPF reported that the per pound rate was increased in some instances from 1.5 cents to 32 cents, or an increase of 2000 percent. The Federation also estimated that the average increase was about $1.00 a year for each subscription.[22]

Second, most publishing sectors share the problem of procuring sufficient advertising revenue. The ethnic press felt that it had been bypassed with regard to government advertising and strongly urged that both federal and provincial government departments, which to some extent have

an obligation to inform newcomers about Canadian ways, offer
much greater assistance.[23] Also, local restrictions for
liquor advertising in Manitoba, Saskatchewan, and Alberta
were felt to be limiting the chance of ethnic papers in
these provinces to compete with similar papers from other
provinces.[24]

Finally, the ethnic press argued that it was burdened
with its own special brand of unfair foreign competition
that closely paralleled that of the English press. Page
news mats, edited and set in Europe and the United States
and completely barren of Canadian content, were placed in
newspapers and used to attract advertising revenue. The
familiar argument was used, that such foreign competition
was grossly unfair and hindered the development of a Canadian consciousness through genuinely Canadian newspapers.[25]
It was also alleged that U.S. publishers showed a complete
disregard for Canadian copyright laws, reproducing material
and selling it in competition with Canadian publications
but at much lower prices. Canadian ethnic publishers also
had to compete with overflow circulation from Europe and
the United States, but this was not considered a critical
problem.

The Senate report dismissed the idea that the government should subsidize the ethnic press indirectly by supply-
ing it with government advertising, but did recommend that
the annual deficit incurred by Canadian Scene should be
financed by the government. Canadian Scene distributes material on Canadian affairs in 15 different languages to
foreign-language publishers.[26]

THE SENATE COMMITTEE REPORT

Thanks to the thorough job performed by the Royal Commission, the Senate Committee had little to do but update
the efforts of its predecessor. The Senate Committee report, which covered the topic of general circulation magazines in 16 pages, mirrored the Royal Commission's study
and extended the analysis only slightly. In general, the
committee found Canadian periodicals to be worse off than
ever, noting that the financial performances of magazines
such as Saturday Night, Maclean's, and Chatelaine were de-
pressingly similar, and concluded that

Canadian magazines are in trouble. The industry
may not be dying, but it is certainly not growing. There are very few Canadian-owned consumer

91

magazines that can claim, with any degree of cer-
tainty, that their survival is assured.[27]

In all, only Time, Reader's Digest, Miss Chatelaine,
and Toronto Calendar Magazine were given clean bills of
health. As any publisher would readily testify, "There
can't be many industries in this country where the odds
are stacked so heavily against success."[28] After observing
that neither circulation nor advertising revenues kept pace
with population increases in Canada, the Senate Committee
stated: "Even at the very best of times, the industry has
been a weak one, and the evidence suggests that it is growing weaker."[29]

The report singles out three main reasons for the industry's state of stagnation. First, overflow circulation
from the United States, which accounts for about 70 percent
of all the magazines purchased in Canada, is the chief factor behind the afflicted state of Canadian magazines. Canadians purchased 147 million copies of U.S. magazines to
45 million copies of Canadian magazines in 1959, and 130.5
million copies of U.S. magazines to 33.8 million copies of
Canadian magazines in 1969--these figures also show that
Canadians are reading fewer magazines. The Senate Committee
commented:

> It is interesting to note, however, that Canada
> appears to be one of the few countries in the
> world which has taken no measures either to dis-
> courage overflow circulation or to encourage a
> domestic periodical industry.[30]

Second, between 1954 and 1968 the share of total advertising
revenues spent on magazines dropped from 4.2 percent to 2.4
percent. The decline in the share of such revenue that was
spent on weekend supplements was even steeper. Advertisers
had switched to other media, especially broadcasting. (See
Appendix C.) And third, once again, Time and Reader's Digest were singled out as unwelcome elements in the periodical industry. Their share of the total advertising revenues
spent in the major consumer magazines had increased from
43 percent in 1958 to 56 percent in 1969. Noting this
trend, the committee felt that " . . . it is reasonable to
anticipate that Time and Reader's Digest will continue to
grab off larger and larger proportions of available revenues."[31] Moreover, the circulation of Reader's Digest had
increased from 1,068,000 in 1960 to 1,448,000 in 1969,
while the circulation of Time had increased from 215,000

in 1960 to about 440,000 in 1969. The committee granted
that both magazines were good corporate citizens, whose
financial success was not wholly attributable to their competitive advantages, but the success of foreign-owned magazines at the expense of Canadian publications was "intolerable." On this basis the committee concluded that

> somehow, despite the economic pitfalls, a way
> must be found to create more equitable competi-
> tive conditions in the Canadian periodical indus-
> try.

> The O'Leary recommendations were sound when
> they were made, and the intent behind them is
> sound today.

> We deeply regret that _Time_ and _Reader's Di-
> gest_ were exempted from the O'Leary legislation.
> It was a bad decision.[32]

It was obvious to the Senators that

> if _Time_ and _Reader's Digest_ are allowed to main-
> tain their present competitive advantage, it will
> become increasingly difficult for existing maga-
> zines to survive, and for new ones to be
> launched.[33]

Since the latter part of the 1950s the Canadian government has been under public pressure to come to grips with
the problems arising from the high degree of foreign investment in Canada, particularly U.S. investment. The committee
also interpreted the magazine problem as symptomatic of the
government's failure to formulate a specific policy cover-
ing foreign investment. The report states:

> We believe that creeping continentalism has
> proceeded far enough in this country. We believe
> the present situation of the magazine industry is
> a perfect example of the dangers of an unexamined
> acceptance of foreign investment.[34]

The Senate Committee then proceeded to advance two
major recommendations, the first of which was that the exemptions now granted _Time_ and _Reader's Digest_ under section
12A of the Income Tax Act should be repealed; this proposal
is exactly in accordance with the Royal Commission's origi-

nal intentions. The Senators argued that even if both magazines continued to operate in Canada, competition would be, at least, more equitable. The logic of Canada's major publishers was dismissed as being predicated on the "effects among _existing_ advertisers in _existing_ magazines." The committee also argued that any economic dislocation would be immediate and short-term and would not compare with the harmful long-term consequences of allowing _Time_ and _Reader's Digest_ to squeeze out existing Canadian publications and preclude the establishment of any new ones. Lastly, the committee believed the magazine industry to be flexible enough to capitalize on the new competitive situation and to occupy quickly any vacuum left by _Time_ and _Reader's Digest_.[35]

Special note must be made of Senator Beaubien's dissenting opinion, in which he emphasized the counterproductive effects of this proposal.[36] He argued that it was unrealistic to expect Canadian companies, which were subject to the highest corporation tax in the free world, to pay for advertising out of after-tax dollars. Beaubien also believed that _Time_'s advertisers were aiming at a section of the public not covered by any other Canadian magazine. He accepted the arguments expressed by the Magazine Advertisers Bureau members and _Toronto Calendar Magazine_ as valid and conclusive.

Beaubien was quite sensitive to the interests of Quebec and was greatly impressed with _Reader's Digest_'s involvement in that province, where it maintained a staff of 396 and provided employment to another 900 Quebecers; if the committee's proposals were enacted, _Time_ and _Reader's Digest_ would get out of Canada. Beaubien stated: "Certainly, in my view, putting a large number of people out of work is not a solution."[37] Senator Beaubien also felt that the real problem was not _Time_ and _Reader's Digest_, but other competing media. The total national advertising market in Canada for 1969 was $300 million, which was distributed as shown in Table 5.2.

Together, _Time_ and _Reader's Digest_ accounted for 56 percent of the $26.7 million spent on magazine advertising (_Time_ took in $9.5 million while _Reader's Digest_ took in $5.1 million). Beaubien found this insignificant when viewed in relation to the total amount spent by advertisers in Canada. He concluded: "Television has been the big gainer, and I do not see much relief for the Canadian magazines unless some way is found of getting rid of the idiot box."[38]

TABLE 5.2

Distribution of Advertising Revenue among the Media

Media		Percent	Millions of Dollars
Television		42.7	128.1
Newspapers	26.6-79.8	34.4	103.2
Newspaper supplements	7.8-23.4		
Radio		14.0	42.0
Magazines		8.9	26.7
Total		100.0	300.0

Source: Senate Debates, 1 (December 9, 1970), 311.

If the first recommendation proved ineffective, and
Time and Reader's Digest continued to profit while Canadian
magazines continued to decline, then the second recommendation of the committee was that, as a condition of publishing
in Canada, both magazines should be required to sell 75 percent of their stock in the Canadian subsidiaries to Canadian
residents and have Canadian residents make up at least 75
percent of their officers and directors.[39]
The committee justified this proposal for truly Canadi-
anizing the two publications by pointing to government
policy regarding broadcasting, newspapers, uranium, banks,
and railroads, which provided ample precedent of required
Canadian equity participation. The Senators pointed out
the "fairness" of the recommendation, which would ultimately
result in two healthy magazines, heavily Canadian in editorial content, and overwhelmingly Canadian in ownership.
The Senators were quite mindful that their proposals,
if implemented, would invite economic retaliation from the
United States, yet they waved aside the commercial calculus
of Canada's major publishers and adamantly reasserted the
need for a unique and vibrant periodical press of singularly
Canadian content. To have done otherwise, they said, would
have been a subordination of the national interest to the
business concerns of a group made up of two foreign publishers and a section of Canada's magazine industry.

THE REACTION TO THE REPORT

In spite of its drastic proposals the Senate report generated little excitement among magazine publishers. Reacting somewhat indifferently, E. P. Zimmerman, the president of Reader's Digest, expressed his confidence that the federal government would simply shelve the part of the report that dealt with consumer periodicals.[40] John Bassett, publisher of the Toronto Telegram, viewed the recommendations as an unjust attempt to impose retroactive legislation on foreign publications that actually aided Canadian magazines in their quest for the advertisers' dollar.[41] In the Senate, David Walker let loose with a scathing clause-by-clause attack on Davey's "gross, cruel criticism" of Time and Reader's Digest.[42]

If we turn to the newspaper editorials we find that the Toronto Telegram flatly came out against curtailing the advantages bestowed on the two foreign magazines.[43] Davey's stand was endorsed by the Edmonton Journal, and the Calgary Herald expressed its support in these words:

> The Committee is on more solid ground in advocating removal of special tax privileges for Time magazine and Reader's Digest . . . certainly, this form of competition for Canadian advertising dollars can be considered inimical to successful domestic magazine publication.[44]

The Ottawa Journal comments:

> But in general there is a welcome atmosphere of help for the underdog in the report. We admire its endorsation of Gratton O'Leary's support nine years ago of small Canadian magazines against Time and Reader's Digest.[45]

Naturally, the Toronto Star supported Davey's proposals; Beland H. Honderich, president and publisher of the Star, said:

> I fail to see why American publications should continue to enjoy privileged status in Canada. . . . The so-called Canadian editions of Time and Reader's Digest contribute little or nothing to the discussion of Canadian affairs by Canadians . . . the law should recognize the truth of the late Henry Luce's statement that Time

magazine is an American and not a Canadian publication.[46]

The Globe and Mail, which had all along objected to
any government action that tended to limit the freedom of
advertisers or hamper the circulation of foreign magazines
in Canada, came out strongly in favor of Davey's recommendations.

Ten years ago Time and the Digest accounted for
43 per cent of the advertising revenue received
by all major consumer magazines in Canada. By
1969 they had built their share up to 56 per cent.
And it wasn't just the national Canadian magazines under fire. Time was publishing 12 regional editions on a regular basis, so that it
was skimming off not only national advertising
but local advertising that might have gone to
regional Canadian magazines. The legislation
designed to protect Canadian magazines is vastly
more effective in protecting Time and the Digest.
Indeed, by executing their U.S. competitors, it
had placed them in the unique position of being
the only magazines in the country which got most
of their editorial matter cheap, from across the
border, and thus were in a unique preferred position to compete with Canadian magazines. To op-
pose this was not to favour nationalism but to
attack special privilege.[47]

It should also be noted that the House of Commons
Standing Committee on External Affairs and the Liberal Convention both recommended that Time and Reader's Digest lose
their exemptions.[48]

NOTES

1. Senate Debates, 1 (November 19, 1968), 547.
2. Ibid., February 4, 1969, p. 943.
3. Ibid., p. 944.
4. Ibid., p. 955.
5. Ibid., p. 156.
6. Ibid., p. 956.
7. Ibid., March 27, 1969, p. 1268.
8. For a short biography of each committee member, see
the Toronto Star, December 9, 1970, p. 8.

9. Toronto _Star_, December 10, 1970, p. 11.

10. _Report of the Special Senate Committee on Mass Media_, 1 (Ottawa: Queen's Printer, 1970), viii.

11. _Proceedings of the Special Committee on Mass Media_, no. 21 (Ottawa: Queen's Printer), pp. 44-47.

12. _Toronto Calendar Magazine_ submission, ibid., March 1970, pp. 56-58.

13. _Senate Debates_, April 28, 1971, p. 932.

14. Ibid., p. 931.

15. _Proceedings of the Senate Committee_, vol. 20, p. 73.

16. Submissions of _Time_ and _Reader's Digest_ to the Senate Committee.

17. Proceedings of the Senate Committee, op. cit., vol. 1, Chap. 3, pp. 153-68.

18. The Senate Committee report simply states that the ethnic press comprises more than 100 publications. _Senate Committee_, vol. 1, p. 179. Kirschbaum, president of the CEPF, referred to more than 100 newspapers in his oral brief before the committee. _Proceedings of the Senate Committee_, no. 18, p. 9.

19. Ibid., p. 1.

20. Ibid.

21. Ibid., O'Leary Commission, pp. 14-16.

22. Ibid., p. 7.

23. Ibid., pp. 7-9.

24. National Publishers Ltd. brief, _Hearings of the Royal Commission on Publications_, vol. 10, pp. 32-33; Canada Press Club of Winnipeg brief, vol. 10, p. 25.

25. Ibid., vol. 10, pp. 24, 29.

26. _Senate Committee_, op. cit., vol. 1, p. 182.

27. Ibid., p. 153.

28. Ibid., p. 155.

29. Ibid., p. 156.

30. Ibid., p. 157.

31. Ibid.

32. Ibid., pp. 163-64.

33. Ibid., p. 164.

34. Ibid., p. 163.

35. For Davey's justification of his proposals see _Senate Committee_, vol. 1, pp. 164-68; _Senate Debates_, December 9, 1970, pp. 306-10; April 28, 1971, pp. 916-40.

36. For the explanation of Beaubien's dissent see _Senate Debates_, December 9, 1970, pp. 310-11.

37. Ibid., vol. 1, p. 311.

38. Ibid., p. 311.

39. _Senate Committee_, vol. 1, p. 166.

40. Toronto _Star_, December 10, 1970, p. 11.

41. Ibid.
42. Senate Debates, February 3, 1971, pp. 466-74.
43. Cited by Davey in Senate Debates, April 28, 1971, p. 924.
44. Ibid., p. 924.
45. Ibid., p. 924.
46. Toronto Star, December 10, 1970, p. 11.
47. Senate Debates, April 28, 1971, p. 924.
48. House of Commons Debates, December 11, 1970, p. 1963.

6

POLITICS AND CULTURE

The issue we wish to discuss in this chapter is why successive Canadian governments have shied away from introducing policies with respect to periodicals that are consistent with the policies applied to other key sectors of the mass media. In short, we argue that the treatment of Time and Reader's Digest provides a gap in what is otherwise a consistent government posture toward the mass media. If this is so, is it because these two foreign companies have been able to exercise special influence on the formulation of Canadian policy, or is there some other reason for their preferred treatment? What policies can now reasonably be introduced? These are some of the questions that we will now examine.

Since Confederation in 1867 Canadian governments have produced no consistent policy toward foreign investment comparable, let us say, to that of Japan. Instead an incremental and ad hoc approach has been taken whereby an assortment of policies has been introduced from time to time to meet particular circumstances.[1] The announcement of the federal government's policy on foreign takeovers of Canadian firms in May 1972 is a further example of the incremental approach, leaving the impression that, if this is not enough, further steps can be taken.[2]

However, an examination of the major laws and regulations affecting foreign investment in Canada as of 1972 shows that most of them can be divided into three major categories: those related to communications and the mass media, those related to financial institutions, and those related to the resource industries.[3] For example, special provisions about Canadian ownership and/or content are con-

tained in the Broadcasting Act, the Telesat Canada Act, the
directions given to the Canadian Radio-Television Commission (C.R.T.C.), the Bank Act, the Canadian and British
Insurance Companies Act, the Loan Companies Act, the Trust
Companies Act, the Investment Companies Act, the Canada
Mining Regulations, the Canada Oil and Gas Land Regulations,
and the Northern Mineral Exploration Assistance Regulations.
In addition, there are provisions in the Income Tax Act
that prescribe special treatment to Canadian-owned firms
with respect to a number of items, including the nondeducti-
bility of advertising expenses for advertisements in newspapers and periodicals that are not Canadian.

The basic philosophy behind these laws and regulations
is difficult to determine, but an implied philosophy appears
to suggest that successive Canadian governments have decided to treat as "key" sectors of the economy, communications and the mass media, financial institutions, and certain primary resource activities. Transportation and power
should perhaps be added to this list, since a Canadian
presence is felt strongly through the federal government's
ownership of the Canadian National Railway, Air Canada, and
Atomic Energy Canada and provincial government ownership of
hydroelectric facilities. The philosophy that is implied
is that these industries should provide, in some sense,
the infrastructure of the economy, as a task of the government comparable to its responsibilities in education,
health, national defense, and justice.

The concept of the infrastructure, which is much discussed but only vaguely defined for a developed country,
would then involve, among others, a set of activities that
are vital for the basic operation of all enterprises; that
is, transportation, communications, finance, and energy.

Periodicals, the subject of the present discussion,
are a part of one of these key sectors, namely, communications and the mass media. The underlying philosophy here
is based on notions of the importance of a Canadian presence
in the mass media because of the impact of the media on
Canadian culture and society. In Chapter 1 we documented
these views as they have been reported in commissions on
radio and television broadcasting and on book publishing,
as well as on periodicals. Running through these reports
were references to the importance of the media in providing
the communications network necessary for the functioning
of the democracy and for the transmission of Canadian news
and values, particularly in view of the overwhelming proxim-
ity of U.S. media, which through overflow operations could
swamp the competing Canadian media. Since a Canadian cul-

tural identity is deemed to be worthwhile, Canadian policy-makers have justified protectionism on the grounds that the economies of scale associated with U.S. firms serving the Canadian market in addition to their own large market give the U.S. firms a substantial advantage over Canadian firms. Such economies are inherent in media operations where, for example, the production of news or information is concerned. There is a large element of fixed costs in producing the information; the average cost of production declines the more outlets through which this information is passed; once it is produced, the extra cost of using the information in an additional outlet is zero.* Once a news story has been written, the more outlets carry it, the better off the company.

But why, if these advantages exist, do the Canadian media not attempt to sell in the U.S. market so as to gain similar economies? One explanation for this is that the Canadian media, like the Canadian nation-state, have always been fighting to create a distinct identity for themselves in North America. The positive drive to develop things Canadian has reflected the "defensive expansionism" outlook described by H. G. J. Aitken.[14] In other words, it has been felt a sufficient challenge to develop a product or service for the Canadian market, without attempting to sell it in the United States as well. In addition, there has always been a lurking feeling that protectionist sentiment in the United States might retaliate and overwhelm any strong Canadian commercial presence there.

A second possible explanation for the failure of Canadian media to cater to the total North American market is a reflection of the sizes of the two countries: what happens in the United States is of international importance and therefore is part of the international news, which is of interest to Canadians; the same cannot be said for Canadian events. Moreover, other foreign news and events tend to get better coverage in the U.S. media, to which the Canadians turn for news of world events. Again, there appears to have been a preoccupation on the part of Canadian media

---

*For example, in an extreme case, where a firm only had fixed costs, its average costs would decline continuously the larger the output produced. If the firm sold all its output at a given price greater than average cost, then the profit per unit (difference between price and average cost) and its total profits would rise with the number of units sold.

to be inward-looking. In part, this may reflect the nature of Canadian federalism, with its distinct cultural components, English and French, as well as its regional components. Canadian media may have had so much difficulty providing a sense of unity within Canada that they have had little time to devote to topics that would have been of interest to American readers.

Summarizing the argument to this point, we have noted, on the one hand, the underlying forces that tend to undermine the development of distinct Canadian media, and, on the other hand, expressions by Canadians that protection of Canadian media is justified on cultural and political grounds.

There are four main theories of what the mass media should be and do for a nation-state. These are the "authoritarian," "libertarian " "social responsibility," and "soviet-totalitarian" theories, the characteristics of which are shown in Table 6.1.[5]

Aspects of both the libertarian and social responsibility theories are found in Canadian policy.[6] The libertarian theory makes a strong case for freedom of the media from government control, in order that the national goals of the media can be fulfilled. The social responsibility theory qualifies the concept of freedom of the media by stating that freedom carries concomitant obligations to society to service the political system, enlighten the public, and safeguard the liberties of individuals. To the extent that the media recognize their responsibilities, the social responsibility approach would be satisfied by the libertarian approach; but if the media are deficient in these responsibilities, under the social responsibility theory adjustments must be made directly or indirectly by government.

The pertinent parts of these theories, for the present discussion, are the roles the media are expected to perform. Major roles, besides the cultural ones mentioned above, include those of independent critics of government and educators and informers of the citizens, who will thereby be able to act responsibly toward government. It would then appear that there are two circumstances that might undermine the satisfactory performance of these political functions: the control of media ownership in a few hands, and the foreign ownership of media. Concentrated control of ownership might lead to a situation whereby the media and the government were too closely allied, or whereby there would not be a large enough number of the "diverse and antagonistic" voices mentioned by the Senate Committee to fulfill their function.[7] Foreign ownership of the media, on the other

TABLE 6.1

Four Social Theories as They Apply to the Mass Media

Characteristics	Authoritarian	Libertarian	Social Responsibility	Soviet-Totalitarian
Time and place of development	16th and 17th century England; widely adopted and still practiced in many places	England and United States after 1688; influential elsewhere	United States in the 20th century	Soviet Union, although some of the same things were done by Nazis and Italians
Philosophical basis	Philosophy of absolute power of monarch, his government, or both	Writings of Milton, Locke, Mill, and general philosophy of rationalism and natural rights	Writing of W. E. Hocking, Commission on Freedom of Press, media codes, and practitioners	Marxist-Leninist-Stalinist thought, with mixture of Hegel and 19th century Russian thinking
Chief purpose	To support and advance the policies of the government in power and to service the state	To inform, entertain, and sell, but chiefly to help discover truth and check on government	To inform, entertain, and sell, but chiefly to raise conflict to the plane of discussion	To contribute to the success and continuance of the Soviet socialist system and especially to the dictatorship of the party
Criterion of availability to the individual	A royal patent or similar permission	Economic means	Something to say	Loyal and orthodox party membership
Control	Government patents, guilds, licensing, sometimes censorship	By "self-righting process of truth" in "free market place of ideas," and by courts	Community opinion, consumer action, professional ethics	Surveillance and economic or political action of government
Limitations	No criticism of political machinery and officials in power	No defamation, obscenity, indecency, wartime sedition	No serious invasion of recognized private rights and vital social interests	No criticism of party objectives, as distinguished from tactics
Ownership	Private or public	Chiefly private	Private unless government has to take over to insure public service	Public
Role	Instruments for effecting government policy, though not necessarily government-owned	Instruments for checking on government and meeting other needs of society	Instruments of social responsibility; if they are not, someone must see to it that they become so	State-owned and closely controlled, existing solely as arm of state

Source: F. S. Siebert, T. Peterson, and W. Schramm, *Four Theories of the Press* (Chicago: University of Illinois, 1956), p. 7.

hand, might lead to a situation whereby foreign interests
act as a major critic of government and provide the educational and informational services to the citizens. The
pressures to which these foreign interests are subject in
their own country might not coincide with the best interests of the citizens. This is not to argue that foreign
interests do not or should not influence domestic citizens
and governments, but that it would be an undesirable situation if foreign interests, representing a different value
system, became the predominant influence-makers.

Apart from the more culturally oriented arguments in
favor of Canadian ownership and content of the media, it
would seem that these political functions also argue in
support of providing some protection for domestic media.
Moreover, it is because of the overwhelming neighborly
presence of the U.S. media that some protection is required
in the Canadian case. This does not mean that U.S. media
influences should be kept out of Canada, but rather that,
partly because of these influences, there should be a strong
Canadian presence as well. Without overt action to assure
a strong Canadian media, there might be none at all.

Lest it be felt that Canada is alone in arguing this
viewpoint, it should be noted that the Royal Commission
did survey the approach taken to overflow and byproduct
circulation in other countries,[8] and concluded that

> With the exception of Canada . . . by-product
> publishing is not a threat to the existence of
> the periodical press in any of the countries
> examined by the Commission.
>   All countries subject to overflow circula-
> tion have enacted measures which provide a degree
> of protection for their domestic periodicals.[9]

This survey records a multitude of ways in which protection is given, including censorship, subsidy, preferential tax rates, and reduced postal rates. The situation of
Ireland with regard to the United Kingdom provides probably
the closest parallel to Canada and the United States. Ireland assists its periodical press in three ways: through
censorship, subsidies, and a per copy duty on periodicals
imported in bulk for newsstand sale.[10]

Although there were no real parallel situations to that
of Canadian editions of American magazines, the Royal Commission's survey showed that there were plenty of precedents
in other countries to support its case for providing some
form of assistance to Canadian periodicals.

It should also be noted that the Canadian government recognizes a responsibility to Canadian culture in other ways that relate to the media. Subsidies and other forms of financial support are provided to Canadian artists and authors, with, for example, the Canada Council and the National Film Board playing a key role in this area. Interestingly enough, neither the Royal Commission nor the Senate Committee referred to the money spent, approximately $2 million in 1968, on the publication of government periodicals intended to promote things Canadian. Certainly there has been no attempt on the part of the Canadian government to integrate the administration of its expenditure on government periodicals with government policy toward private periodicals, both of which have related objectives.

A recent study has examined the role of nontechnical periodicals produced by government departments.[11] None of these periodicals carries commercial advertising, although this practice is permitted by Treasury Board. Twenty-seven of them were classified as being intended for national circulation, four for international circulation, and twenty-nine for internal departmental circulation. (See Appendix F.) The total annual cost of these publications was estimated to be about $2 million, with the circulation for each periodical ranging between 350 and 2 million. These circulation data are not very meaningful because most of the publications are distributed free, usually without the recipients requesting them. Only six periodicals solicit paid subscriptions, and only in the case of one periodical do subscriptions account for more than half the total circulation.

The evaluation made of these government periodicals is that, with few exceptions, the content is dull and the quality of writing is poor, although the layout and design are quite respectable and the quality of paper used is good.

While government periodicals do not compete with privately owned periodicals for advertising, they do promote Canadian activities; indeed, because of their origin, they may provide a too uncritical view of Canada. However, since the government participates in the periodical industry to the tune of $2 million annually, it is desirable that it formulate some objective and attempt to achieve it, which does not appear to be the case at the present time.

So far we have argued that the Canadian government has, in effect, designated certain activities as key sectors of the economy on which restrictions on ownership and content should be placed. The mass media are one such sector. The rationale for restrictions on the mass media reflect both cultural considerations and the political functions that the media are supposed to perform. In the absence of such restrictions it is felt that U.S. media interests would overwhelm competing Canadian firms. Ownership and content requirements have therefore been devised for Canadian radio and television broadcasting and ownership requirements have been made for Canadian newspapers. Policies toward Canadian book publishing are now being developed at the federal level and by the Ontario government.

In the field of periodical publishing a policy has been devised that has the effect of treating two foreign periodicals as Canadian, namely Time and Reader's Digest. In the light of Canada's other policies toward the mass media, is there any justification for allowing Time and Reader's Digest to engage in byproduct circulation in Canada? Do they, for example, make an outstanding political or cultural contribution to Canada that they would not make if they were merely allowed to engage in overflow circulation, as is the treatment accorded to other foreign periodicals? The issue then is not whether Time and Reader's Digest should be available in Canada or not at all, but rather whether Time and Reader's Digest should be available in Canada as byproduct circulation as opposed to overflow circulation. If there is no singular contribution that the Canadian editions of Time and Reader's Digest make to Canada that would not be made by allowing Canadian editions of Newsweek, Business Week, Playboy, or True Confessions, which are restricted to overflow circulation, then there is no consistent reason why Time and Reader's Digest should not be subjected to similar treatment.

A glance at the contribution to Canada claimed by Reader's Digest is shown in Table 6.2, which provides some interesting information. Over a period in which there were 72 issues of Reader's Digest (monthly from 1963 to 1968), about once every three months, on the average, there was an article by a Canadian author; about once every three months there was an article that probably had already been published by a Canadian publisher then adapted by Reader's Digest (necessarily Canadian only in the sense that it was supplied by a publishing house in Canada); once every two months there was an article about Canada or Canadians (this ratio would be improved if the articles in other categories were about Canada or Canadians as well); once every three months there was an article that was considered Canadian because the Montreal editorial staff had worked on it. This breakdown of so-called Canadian articles does not appear to provide a strong argument in favor of a Canadian edition of

TABLE 6.2

Canadian Articles Published in the Canadian
English-Language Editions of Reader's Digest, 1963-68

Category	Number Published
Articles written by Canadian authors	27
Articles published by arrangement with other Canadian publishers	22
Articles about Canada or Canadians drawn from the international editorial pool	37
Articles specially adapted for the Canadian editions by the Montreal editorial staff, from material of universal interest drawn from the international editorial pool	24

Source: Extracted from material prepared by Reader's Digest for presentation to the Special Senate Committee on Mass Media, 1969.

Reader's Digest. More important, it is doubtful whether there would be many less articles about Canada or Canadians with overflow circulation of Reader's Digest, since some of the articles mentioned in Table 6.2 would probably have appeared in the regular edition. Certainly, in terms of content there is little to justify byproduct circulation of Reader's Digest.

In the case of Time, the same type of argument can be made. With overflow circulation some information about Canada would still appear in Time's pages--even the banana republics get some coverage--and the Canadian content of Time's Canadian edition does not justify its preferential treatment.

If Time and Reader's Digest do not make a significant contribution to Canadian culture and politics, then the reason for their preferred status under the Income Tax Act would seem to reflect the influence on Canadian political decisions that these two firms have managed to exert or to have had exerted on their behalf. Our analysis in the earlier chapters has indicated the ways in which these two firms have attempted to influence the formulation of Canadian periodical policy through briefs and submissions,

through editorials or articles in their magazines, and
through the persuasive influence of U.S. government officials at times when other issues were being negotiated between Canada and the United States. Recently, however,
the influence of the Magazine Advertising Bureau (M.A.B.)
seems to have been important. This group was organized on
the urgings of Reader's Digest in the wake of the Income
Tax Amendment. At the time of the Senate Committee's hearings all Canadian members of the M.A.B. vigorously supported
the existing treatment given to their fellow members, Time
and Reader's Digest. It appears, then, that the foreign
periodicals, having been instrumental in establishing a
trade association in Canada, then managed to convince their
Canadian fellow members that no changes to existing periodical policy were desirable.

In discussing the policy options that are now open to
Canada, it should be noted that there is a general concern
about the operation within Canada of foreign-owned firms.
This concern centers on the fact that the key decisionmaking
powers rest in the hands of foreign nationals who are subject to the political environment and value system of a
foreign country. In the mass media field this is well il-
lustrated in the case of Reader's Digest.[12]

The decisionmaking center for the worldwide operations
of Reader's Digest is situated in New York State. Although
there is a vice-president in charge of international operations to whom senior executives of its foreign affiliates
report, DeWitt Wallace, as president of Reader's Digest,
maintains direct contact with selected subsidiaries, particularly Canada. To ensure that the operating executives
of the foreign subsidiaries project the Reader's Digest
image and philosophy, most of the materials published in
all of the foreign editions are obtained from the central
editorial pool maintained in the United States. The parent
company exercises management control over its worldwide
operations through these editorial arrangements and by its
direction to all affiliates regarding dividend policy.

It is obvious that Reader's Digest operates in a very
sensitive area of Canadian life, and for this reason it has
to take careful note of Canadian feelings. It is editorial
policy and control that poses a real problem for Canada.
News media have long been recognized as having an important
influence on people's views and opinions of events, and in
a very real sense the media interpret what it is to be a
Canadian. In this context, the close control of the editorial content of Reader's Digest by the parent company and
its insistence that articles be contributed to a central

pool based in the United States, along with the general rule that the majority of articles must first appear in the U.S. edition, not only limits the effectiveness of its Canadian contribution but also serves to place a U.S. bias on the range of selection available. While the stated policy of the parent company is to shy away from politically oriented subjects, the many articles on such topics as the success of Nationalist China, the threat posed by Red China, and the inevitability of free enterprise in the communist world, seem to contradict this position.

POLICY OPTIONS

In view of the sociocultural role of the mass media in society, and in the light of the impact byproduct circulation has on Canada, we will now consider three possible policy options with respect to the Canadian periodical industry.[13]

No Change

Under a policy of no change the tax status of Time and Reader's Digest remains as is. This policy recommendation was put forward by members of M.A.B. before the Senate Committee. Before proceeding to highlight some of their key arguments it should be noted that on the basis of advertising earnings Reader's Digest and Time finance approximately 50 percent of the operating costs of M.A.B. The key points stressed in favor of continuing the exemption status included the following.

First, the withdrawal of the exemption might prompt Reader's Digest and Time to close up shop in Canada. If this were to happen there would be fewer Canadian magazines, and the cost of advertising in them would increase because the Canadian base of distribution would become smaller. In short, magazines would be a less attractive medium in which to advertise, while the other competing media such as television and newspapers would be correspondingly more attractive.

Second, the M.A.B. argued that there was no assurance that making it more expensive to advertise in Reader's Digest and Time would stop advertisers from patronizing these two magazines. The net effect of this might be fewer advertising dollars spent on other Canadian magazines. This would be particularly true in the case of Time, most of the major

Canadian advertisers in which are subsidiaries of large international firms that receive a significant discount (10 percent) when they advertise in both the U.S. and Canadian editions. If the tax exemption were removed, Reader's Digest and Time would not suffer much in terms of loss of advertising revenue whether they continued or ceased to maintain their Canadian operations.

Third, it was pointed out by the M.A.B. that both Time and Reader's Digest were good corporate citizens, that their success should be attributed to their excellent products and not merely to the competitive advantage they enjoyed by being affiliated to their parent company, and that the final arbiters of their profitability were their customers, both readers and advertisers, who continued to favor them with their business.

The fourth reason offered for not repealing the tax-exempt status of Reader's Digest and Time was probable retaliation from the United States. R. A. McEacher put forward the following argument to the Senate Committee on Mass Media:

> Remember that in view of the enormous American penetration of Canada, a great many of the big advertising decisions are not made in Canada, but in head offices in the United States. If the Government of Canada were to go ahead and make a move against the two publications named, this would set off a typhoon of criticism. We would be charged with anti-Americanism and all sorts of things; so certainly for a time we would suffer.[14]

It is interesting to note that the M.A.B. submission declined to discuss the sociocultural significance of national magazines. Its emphasis was on magazines as a "national advertising medium" and on the fear that without Reader's Digest and Time the advertisers would not be able to achieve the necessary coverage through general circulation magazines. In short, the members of the M.A.B. argued that their commonality of interest was advertising revenue and that this could best be achieved by working together.

One might conjecture that the advertising dollars realized through magazine sales is not the entire reason these U.S. magazines operate in Canada. For example, Reader's Digest, in addition to producing the Reader's Digest in the English and the French languages, produces "English and French editions of Reader's Digest Condensed Books; dictionaries; atlases and other reference works;

other books on a wide variety of subjects; terrestrial globes; and phonograph record albums."[15] It was also noted that

> During the past ten years the Company (Reader's Digest) has increased the sales of products other than its magazines from 34.4% to 51.9% of its total sales. The success of this diversification program is partly attributable to possession by the Company of the largest magazine subscription list in Canada.[16]

This point was overlooked by both the Royal Commission and the Senate Committee.

Good corporate citizenship based on vague guidelines that carry no legal sanction is not a sufficient reason for granting tax exemption to Time and Reader's Digest. Moreover, it was argued by nonmembers of the M.A.B. that the Canadian periodical industry could compete if the tax-exempt status of Time and Reader's Digest were removed. One nonmember of the M.A.B., the editor of Executive magazine, expressed the following opinion:

> Canada now needs a strong national press as much as it needed the Canadian Pacific Railway in the late 1800's. That press now has the talent, insight and experience necessary to serve the people of Canada in a way that no foreign publications can. But we need the chance to do it—to prove it. Given the amount of advertising dollars now going to Time and Reader's Digest, it is certain that we'll be given neither the opportunity nor the tools.[17]

In recent years a few Canadian periodical firms have established foreign operations, notably Maclean-Hunter in the United States. The possibility of U.S. retaliation, mentioned by R. A. McEacher of Maclean-Hunter, may account for the reversal of position taken by this firm between the time of the Royal Commission and the time of the Senate Committee. Maclean-Hunter has a U.S. subsidiary in Chicago, Maclean-Hunter Publishing Corporation, which publishes five business periodicals in the United States. In 1966 this company purchased 100 percent of National Market Reports Inc. of Chicago.[18]

We take the position that for sociocultural reasons the mass media field should be identified as a key sector of the economy, and therefore we reject this policy option of "no change."

Removal of the Tax-Exempt Status
of *Time* and *Reader's Digest*

Both the Royal Commission and the Senate Committee viewed the periodical industry as something more than an economic producing unit. In the words of the committee, "the consumer magazine segment of the industry is by far the most important segment in terms of our cultural survival. It is also the segment which, because of subsidized foreign competition faces the greatest difficulties."[19] Since magazines have the potential of being national in scope like television and radio, it is vital that the undermining influence of byproduct circulation be eliminated in order to promote a strong Canadian presence. For this reason, the Senate Committee reintroduced the Royal Commission recommendation that "the exemptions now granted *Time* and *Reader's Digest* under Section 12A of the Income Tax Act be repealed, and the sooner the better."[20]

Although the members of the M.A.B. argued against this policy option on the grounds that it would have a disastrous effect on the periodical industry, the evidence collected by the Senate Committee indicates that this need not be the case. The committee felt that the Canadian magazine industry "would be a lot sicker" had Section 12A not been introduced in 1965, and that the business press in Canada was flourishing as a direct result of it. Moreover, they argued that if section 12A had been applied to *Reader's Digest* and *Time* when it was first introduced, more Canadian magazines would be in business.

The critical point to consider is the future of the Canadian magazine industry. The removal of the exemption would make competition more equitable and hence strengthen existing Canadian magazines, and help to promote the entry of new Canadian magazines. The continued existence and modicum of success of such magazines as *Chatelaine*, *Maclean's*, and *Saturday Night* shows that there is both an audience and the Canadian talent necessary to foster a Canadian periodical industry.

In short, this policy option does not restrict itself to a consideration of advertising revenues in the way that the first policy option does; it recognizes the sociocultural significance of periodicals in the national context and expresses confidence in the ability of Canadian magazine firms to make a real contribution, particularly if the competitive advantages enjoyed by Reader's Digest and Time were eliminated. Indeed, this policy recommendation would merely establish consistency in Canadian policy toward the mass media.

Although we favor this consistent approach, its rejection by successive Canadian governments in recent years suggests to us that, for various political reasons, it is unlikely to be implemented. For this reason we do not believe that this is a viable policy option for the 1970s.

Canadianization

The third policy approach would be aimed at exploiting the presence of Time and Reader's Digest to the greater benefit of Canada. This might be done by applying to magazines the ownership policies that are applied to Canadian banks and the content policies that are applied to Canadian television. Greater Canadian ownership of the Canadian operations of Reader's Digest and Time would have the effect of assuring greater Canadian influence, and awareness of Canada, on the editorial policies of the magazines; stipulating certain guidelines for Canadian content would ensure that Canadian cultural and political interests were adequately promoted. This would encourage the reporting of Canadian and foreign events from a Canadian perspective.

This policy might stipulate that 75 percent of the stock of the two companies must be held by Canadians and that the majority of the officers and directors must be Canadian residents. Reader's Digest has already gone part way in satisfying the above criteria: 30 percent of its Canadian subsidiary's stock is held by Canadian residents; the majority of its directors are Canadians; and the president is a Canadian.

This policy option could lead to the creation of two new Canadian magazines, provided that the content policies that are now applied to television are also applied to periodicals. In short, this policy is predicated on defining the media as a key sector of the economy. Although this action is retroactive, there is a precedent for it in the treatment of Famous Players Canadian Corporation Ltd. and R.K.O. Distributing Corporation (Canada) Ltd., which were forced to sell 80 percent of their Canadian holdings under the direction of the C.R.T.C.[21]

The implementation of the Canadianization policy option would have the effect of eliminating an anomaly in the Cana-

dian mass media field. Reader's Digest and Time would have
to decide between operating on an overflow circulation basis
or adjusting to a situation in which their Canadian affili-
ate operations would have a high degree of editorial auton-
omy. The application of C.R.T.C.-type content regulations
(55 percent of all copy to be basically Canadian in content
and authorship) would promote new editorial departments in
Canada, and thus opportunities for Canadian creative talent.
Although the editorial costs for these magazines would increase, some of the Canadian material might be sold to
Time and Reader's Digest in the United States for use in
the United States and in their worldwide operations. In
addition, this structural reorganization would have the effect of putting competing Canadian-produced periodicals on
a more equal basis. A prime responsibility of the Canadian
directors would be to ensure that the content provisions
were being satisfied by the two firms.
    Over a decade has passed since the Canadian government
first gave serious consideration to curbing the operations
of Time and Reader's Digest. In the intervening years two
major government studies, the Royal Commission on Publications and the Senate Committee Report on the Mass Media,
have focused national attention on the plight of Canadian
periodicals that compete with "foreign" publications. The
two reports were unanimous in their observations: Time and
Reader's Digest affected detrimentally the well-being of
the Canadian periodical industry and their special status
in Canada should end. By as early as the 1920s, it had become evident that the Canadian government viewed the communications industry as a critical vehicle in promoting Canadianism and for this reason it merited special assistance.
In the light of the findings of our study, the authors
recommend a policy of "Canadianization" for Reader's Digest
and Time.

                              NOTES

    1. A comparative approach can be found in I. A. Lit-
vak and C. J. Maule, Foreign Investment: The Experience of
Host Countries (New York: Praeger Publishers, 1970).
    2. House of Commons Debates, May 2, 1972, pp. 1828-29.
The impression that further steps might be taken was given
in a television press conference given by the Minister of
National Revenue and the Minister of Industry, Trade and
Commerce on May 2, 1972.
    3. Selected Readings in Laws and Regulations Affect-
ing Foreign Investment in Canada, Foreign Investment Divi-

sion, Office of Economics, Department of Industry, Trade and Commerce (Ottawa: Queen's Printer, 1972).

4. H. G. J. Aitkin, "Domestic Expansionism: The State and Economic Growth in Canada," in Aitken, ed., The State and Economic Growth (New York: Social Science Research Council, 1959), pp. 79-114.

5. F. S. Siebert, T. Peterson, and W. Schramm, Four Theories of the Press (Chicago: University of Illinois, 1956).

6. Further treatment of this topic can be found in E. Black, "Canadian Policy and the Mass Media," Canadian Journal of Economics, 1, no. 2 (May 1968), 368-79.

7. Report of the Special Senate Committee on Mass Media (Ottawa: Queen's Printer, 1970), p. 6.

8. Report on the Royal Commission on Publications (Ottawa: Queen's Printer, 1961), pp. 203-16.

9. Ibid., p. 215.

10. Ibid., p. 208.

11. "Report on Government Non-Technical Periodical Publishing," memo, Information Canada, Ottawa, 1971.

12. This case is treated in detail in I. A. Litvak, C. J. Maule, and R. D. Robinson, Dual Loyalty: Canadian-U.S. Business Arrangements (Toronto: McGraw-Hill, 1971), pp. 98-111.

13. Variations of some of these proposals are discussed in Senate Committee, vol. 1, Chap. 3.

14. Senate Committee, op. cit., p. 162.

15. The Reader's Digest Association (Canada) Ltd., Prospectus (Montreal: Greenshields Inc., 1968), p. 3.

16. Ibid., p. 4.

17. Senate Committee, op. cit., p. 162.

18. See Annual Report, Maclean-Hunter Ltd., Toronto, 1971, pp. 4, 24.

19. Senate Committee, op. cit., p. 163.

20. Ibid., p. 165.

21. Ibid., p. 166.

PARTICIPANTS APPEARING BEFORE THE
ROYAL COMMISSION ON PUBLICATIONS

Ottawa (38)

Canadian Publishers (6)

Consolidated Press Limited, Maclean-Hunter Publishing
Company, Montreal Standard Publishing Company, Poirier Bes-
sette and Cie. Ltée, Public Printing and Stationery, Toronto
Star.

Foreign Publishers (7)

Family Circle, Fawcett Publications Inc., Gordon and
Gotch (Canada) Ltd., Hearst Corporation, Macfadden Publications Inc., Reader's Digest Association of Canada, Time International of Canada.

Publishers' Associations (8)

L'Association Canadienne des Bibliothécaires de Langue
Francaise, The Book Publishers Association, Business News-
papers Association, Canadian University Press, Canadian
Weekly Newspapers Association, Graphic Arts Industries As-
sociation, Magazine Publishers Association, Periodical Press
Association.

Business Associations (3)

Association of Canadian Advertisers Incorporated, Association of Industrial Advertisers, Canadian Association
of Advertising Agencies.

Other (14)

K. L. Brown, Canadian Association of Consumers, Canadian and Catholic Confederation of Labour, Canadian Institute of Adult Education, Canadian Labour Congress, Canadian Royal Geographical Society, C. Fraser Elliot, French Canadian Association of Education for the Province of Quebec, P. Hailstone, K. Johnston, National Farmers Union, National Gallery of Canada, Radio College of Canada, Graham Spry.

Toronto (35)

Canadian Publishers (11)

Age Publications Ltd., Arthurs-Franklin Publications, Canada Track and Traffic Publishing Company, Maclean-Hunter (Canadian Homes Magazine), Maclean-Hunter (Chatelaine), Maclean-Hunter (Maclean's), Monetary Times Publications, Seccombe House, Southam-Maclean Publications, Toronto Star Limited, University of Toronto Press.

Foreign Publishers (4)

Curtis Publishing Company, Iliffe and Sons, McGraw-Hill Publishing Company, Sponsor Magazine.

Publishers' Associations (5)

Business Papers Editors Association, Canadian Ethnic Press Club, Magazine Publishers Association, Periodical Distributors Association of Canada, The Society for Arts Publications.

Business Associations (4)

Association of Canadian Advertisers Inc., Canadian Association of Advertising Agencies, Dominion Electrohome Industries, John Inglis Company Ltd.

Other (11)

Ralph Allen, Anglican Church of Canada, G. Cadogan,
Canada Council, Canadian Circulation Audit Board, Mrs.
Trent Frayne, Ontario Federation of Printing Trades Unions,
B. T. Richardson, S. J. B. Sugden, Toronto Public Library,
J. L. Wild.

Montreal (31)

Canadian Publishers (6)

Actualité, Montreal Standard Publishing Company, National Business Publications Ltd., Photo-Journal, Rod and
Gun Publishing Company, Wallace Publishing Co.

Foreign Publishers (1)

Newsweek Inc.

Publishers' Associations (3)

L'Association Des Maîtres-Imprimeurs de Montréal Inc.,
Business Paper Editors Association, Employing Printers Association of Montreal.

Business Associations (10)

Agence Canadienne Hachette Ltée., Benjamin News Company,
Canadian Advertising and Sales Clubs, Canadian Pulp and
Paper Association, Chemical Institute of Canada, T. Eaton
Company, Industrial-Safety Service Inc., Meco Limited, Simp-
sons-Sears Limited, Visual Equipment Company.

Other (11)

Canadian Library Association, Federation of Interna-
tional Printing and Trade Unions of the Province of Quebec,
Reginald R. Fife, Julian Huven, Hugh MacLennan, J. E. Mc-
Dougall, Phyllis Lee Peterson, Leslie Roberts, F. R. Scott,
Albert Shea, George J. Wesley.

Quebec (4)

Canadian Publishers (2)

Maclean-Hunter (Chatelaine-La Revue Moderne), Maclean-Hunter (Le Magazine Maclean).

Other (2)

L'Association de Recherches Sur Les Sciences Religieuses et Profanes au Canada, Province of Quebec (Librarian).

Vancouver (17)

Canadian Publishers (4)

Design for Better Living Publications, Magor-Way Press Limited, Mitchell Press Limited, Purchasing in Western Canada.

Foreign Publishers (1)

Miller Freeman Publications.

Publishers' Associations (2)

British Columbia Photo-Engravers Association, The Graphic Arts Association of British Columbia.

Other (10)

Community Arts Council of British Columbia, Jurgen Grohne, Raymond Hall, Pat Hanley, Bruce Hutchison, Stuart Keate, Hugh L. Keenleyside, Freda Nevill, Realm News Service Ltd., University of British Columbia.

Regina (1)

Other (1)

Government of Saskatchewan.

Winnipeg (8)

Canadian Publishers (3)

National Publishers Ltd., The Public Press Ltd., Stovel Advocate Publications Ltd.

Publishers' Associations (2)

Canada Ethnic Press Federation, Canada Press Club of Winnipeg.

Other (3)

Canadian Authors Association (Winnipeg), Canadian Circulation Consultants, Winnipeg Master Printers and Lithographers Association.

Halifax (7)

Canadian Publishers (3)

Dalhousie Review, Dartmouth Free Press, The University Press of New Brunswick.

Business Associations (1)

Halifax Board of Trade

Other (3)

The Catholic Women's League of Canada, C.J.C.H. Ltd., Watson Kirkconnell.

Source: Report of the Royal Commission on Publications (Ottawa: Queen's Printer, 1961), pp. 113-52.

PARTICIPANTS APPEARING BEFORE THE SENATE
COMMITTEE ON THE MASS MEDIA

Periodical Interests (24)

Actualité, Canadian Business Press, Canadian Business
Press Editors Association, Canadian Church Press, The Cana-
dian-Star Weekly, Chatelaine, Graphic Arts Industries Asso-
ciation, International Typographical Union, Les Journaux
Trans-Canada Ltée., Maclean-Hunter Business Publications,
Maclean-Hunter Ltd., Maclean's, Magazine Advertising Bureau,
M. Pierre Peladeau (prés., Quebecor Inc.), Presbyterian
Record, Reader's Digest, Saturday Night, Southam Business
Publications Ltd., Southam Press Ltd., Time, Toronto Life,
Underground Press Roundtable (Georgia Straight) The United
Church Observer, Weekend-Perspectives.

Newspaper Interests (42)

American Newspaper Guild, Armadale Company Ltd. (Regina
Leader-Post, Saskatoon Star Phoenix), Association of English
Media Journalists, John Bassett (Toronto Telegram), W. J.
Blackburn (London Free Press), Brantford Expositor, Calgary
Herald, Canada Ethnic Press Federation, Canadian Daily News-
paper Publishers Association, Canadian Managing Editors' Con-
ference, The Canadian Press, Canadian Scene, Canadian So-
ciety of Professional Journalists, Canadian Weekly Newspa-
pers Association, Corriere Canadese, Paul Desmarais, Le
Droit, Fédération professionnelle des journalistes du Qué
bec, F.P. Publications (Winnipeg Free Press), Fredericton
Gleaner, Free Press Weekly, Halifax Herald, Hamilton Spec-
tator, Les Hebdos du Canada, International Typographical
Union, K. C. Irving Ltd., Montreal Star, Ottawa Journal,
Parliamentary Press Gallery, Peterborough Examiner, La
Presse, Prince Albert Herald, Claude Ryan (Le Devoir),
Southam Press Ltd., St. John Telegraph-Journal, St. John's
Evening Telegram, Thomson Newspapers Ltd., Toronto Globe
and Mail, Toronto Star, University Press Roundtable (McGill
Daily), Vancouver Province, Windsor Star.

Broadcasting Interests (27)

Acadia Broadcasting Company Ltd., Association of Canadian Television and Radio Artists, Broadcast News Ltd., Bushnell Communications Ltd., Canadian Association of Broadcasters, Canadian Cable Television Association, CBC, CFPL Broadcasting Ltd., CHSJ Television, CHUM Ltd., Countryside Holdings Ltd., CRTC, CTV, F.P. Publications Ltd., Jarmain Cable Systems Ltd., K. C. Irving Ltd., Maclean-Hunter Cable TV Limited, Moffat Broadcasting Ltd., Monarch Broadcasting Company Ltd., Radio Futura Ltd., Selkirk Holdings Ltd., Southam Press Ltd., Standard Broadcasting Corporation Ltd., Télémedia (Quebec) Ltée., Télé-Métropole Corporation, Télévision St.-Maurice Inc., Western Broadcasting Company Ltd.

Other Interests (20)

Agricultural Institute of Canada, Earle J. Beattie (Professor of Journalism, University of Western Ontario), Richard Beddoes, Donald Cameron, Canadian Council on Rural Development, Canadian Home and School and Parent-Teacher Federation, Canadian Public Relations Society, CLC, Consumers Association of Canada, Una Maclean Evans, Douglas Fisher (broadcaster and columnist, Toronto Telegram), Jerry Goodis (Advertising Executive), D. H. Henry (Combines Investigation Branch), Indian-Eskimo Association, The Institute of Canadian Advertising, Nicholas Johnson, Eric Kierans, Thelma H. McCormick, T. L. McPhail, Professor Tom Sloan (ex-journalist and head of faculty of communications, Laval University).

Source: Compiled from a list of participants prepared by the Special Senate Committee on Mass Media, 1970.

SOME STATISTICS OF THE
PERIODICAL INDUSTRY IN CANADA

1. The share of media advertising being spent on daily
newspapers and periodicals has declined markedly since 1955,
mainly because of the growth of television advertising.
(See Figure A.1.)
2. Canadian magazines' share of total net advertising
revenue declined from 4.2 percent in 1954 to 2.4 percent in
1968.*

FIGURE A.1

Growth of Media Advertising by Medium, 1950-67

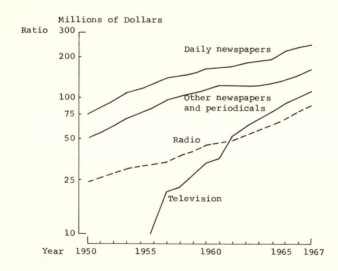

Source: Senate Committee on the Mass Media, Vol. II
(Ottawa: Queen's Printer, 1970), p. 122.

---

*Report of the Special Senate Committee on the Mass
Media, 1 (Ottawa: Queen's Printer, 1970), 156.

TABLE A.1

Net Advertising Revenue by Printed Medium, 1950-69

Year	Daily	National Weekend	Weekly, Bi-Weekly, Etc.	General Circulation	Trade, Technical, Scientific	Agricultural	Controlled Distribution Weekly	Telephone Directory	Other	Total Revenue (in millions of dollars)
1950	60.27	5.13	8.43	7.10	7.61	4.19	--	6.23	1.04	127.5
1951	60.60	5.16	9.28	7.24	7.52	2.79	--	6.09	1.32	140.7
1952	60.26	5.49	9.18	6.97	7.87	2.92	--	5.96	1.35	157.0
1953	60.72	5.42	9.17	6.74	7.83	2.81	--	5.93	1.38	180.8
1954	59.66	5.94	9.14	7.34	7.83	2.52	--	6.24	1.33	194.6
1955	59.88	6.04	9.07	7.40	7.67	2.21	--	6.47	1.21	212.5
1956	59.31	6.12	8.06	7.47	8.60	2.63	--	6.67	1.14	240.1
1957	58.66	6.10	7.70	7.26	9.17	2.49	--	7.50	1.12	249.6
1958	58.44	5.92	7.78	6.82	8.96	2.42	--	8.53	1.13	261.0
1959	58.78	5.43	7.74	6.54	8.90	2.39	--	9.14	1.08	282.9
1960	57.63	5.80	7.81	7.13	8.44	2.18	--	9.71	1.00	294.9
1961	58.31	5.67	7.93	6.63	8.44	1.93	0.23	10.07	0.77	298.7
1962	59.58	5.51	8.06	5.79	7.95	1.79	0.25	10.37	0.70	308.9
1963	59.89	5.44	7.94	5.53	7.96	1.79	0.22	10.50	0.73	313.3
1964	59.80	5.47	8.02	5.44	8.06	1.69	0.28	10.52	0.72	327.6
1965	61.21	4.82	8.17	5.45	8.30	1.17	0.41	9.64	0.83	360.8
1966	61.06	4.52	8.60	5.69	7.59	1.42	0.54	9.66	0.93	384.7
1967	59.11	3.92	10.58	5.66	7.99	1.49	0.44	9.90	0.89	405.7
1968	60.2	4.0	10.8	5.5	6.5	1.4	0.8	10.0	0.8	431.7
1969	61.6	4.0	9.7	5.5	6.4	1.3	0.8	10.0	0.7	481.1

Source: Senate Committee on the Mass Media, 2 (Ottawa: Queen's Printer, 1970), 192-93; Printing, Publishing and Allied Industries (Ottawa: Queen's Printer), D.B.S. 36-203, October 1971, p. 31.

3. Within the print industry, magazines' share of advertising revenue declined from 7.1 percent in 1950 to 5.5 percent in 1969. (See Table A.1.)

4. *Time* and *Reader's Digest* accounted for 56 percent of the net advertising revenue in major consumer magazines in Canada in 1969, up from 43 percent in 1959.* Between 1960 and 1969, *Reader's Digest*'s circulation in Canada increased from 1.1 million to 1.5 million, and *Time*'s from 215,000 to 440,000.**

---

*Ibid., p. 154-55.
**Ibid., p. 158.

READER'S DIGEST: "AN OPEN LETTER
ON A CRUEL DILEMMA"

Dear Reader:

On September 16, 1960, the Government of Canada appointed a Royal Commission to "inquire into" and "make recommendations" concerning certain aspects of the periodical
publishing business in Canada. For months the Royal Commission held hearings in cities across Canada. Representatives
of The Reader's Digest appeared twice before the Commission
and submitted to it massive quantities of pertinent information and evidence. The Commission itself made frequent
requests to the Digest for information, and each request
was complied with promptly, cheerfully and completely.

From the outset it was painfully clear to us of the
Digest that so far as our magazine was concerned the Commission faced a dual problem. On the one hand was the Commission's belief that Canadian consumer magazines needed to be
provided with a measure of "protection" against competition
from periodicals originating outside Canada; and, on the
other hand, was the unique position of the Digest which,
while originating outside Canada, had for 19 years been in-
tegrated into the country. It is staffed by Canadians and
provides employment for more than 1000 Canadian citizens.
Each year it pumps more than $11,000,000 into the Canadian
economy--and each month it brings pleasant and fruitful
hours of reading to some 4,000,000 Canadian readers.

On June 15, 1961, the Prime Minister tabled the Commission's Report in the House of Commons. The Report listed
the main competition facing Canadian magazines as television,
imported magazines or so-called overflow circulation, weekend periodicals and Canadian editions of U.S. magazines,
"probably in that order." But the recommendations of the
Commission had the effect of seriously penalizing only the
elements of fourth priority: "Canadian editions of U.S.
magazines." There are only two of them, one of the two
being The Reader's Digest--the only one with a long and
substantial history of operating in Canada.

On January 22, 1962, the Prime Minister said his Government would ask Parliament to implement the Commission's

recommendations--with, he added, "an important modification." The Commission had recommended, in effect, that any Canadian firm advertising in the Digest be denied the right to deduct any of the cost as a business expense. The Government was proposing that this apply to any new Canadian editions of foreign magazines but that Canadian firms be entitled to deduct half the cost of their advertising in the Digest. Meanwhile, of course, they would continue to deduct the whole cost of advertising placed in other magazines in Canada generally. Even with this modification, the effect of the action contemplated by the Government on The Reader's Digest of Canada would be devastating. From a prosperous, happy and, we believe, useful business, ours would be suddenly reduced to a marginal one. The jobs of many Canadians would be in jeopardy.

If enacted into law by Parliament, the Government's proposal would have the effect, so far as we can now calculate, of increasing the cost of advertising in our magazine by some 40 to 50 percent. Since, in the words of the Commission itself, "advertising is the lifeblood of periodical publishing," this obviously would place the Canadian Digest under a crippling handicap. How long we could carry such a burden--one borne by no other publisher of long standing in Canada--is a matter which gives us most urgent concern.

If the proposal does become law, the Digest in Canada would be faced with a cruel dilemma:

Our first duty would be to you, our readers. We would continue to provide for you each month a fresh issue of the Digest, just as interesting, just as complete, just as entertaining as ever--and, we would earnestly hope, at no increase in price to you. But whether we could continue to produce the copies in Canada under such a burden is doubtful. The alternative, bitterly distasteful to us, would be to revert to the policy of most other American publishers--to supply Canadians with copies from the United States, something we stopped doing nearly two decades ago.

It's the cruelest of dilemmas. Withdrawing from Canada and reverting to the production of Canadian copies in the United States would protect the Digest from the harsh and discriminating economic consequences of the new law; but for the Digest this would involve abandoning its home in Canada and abandoning the 1000 Canadians who depend on it for living and career. For Canada itself, it would involve the loss of our $11,000,000-a-year business and our plans for a bright and expanding future.

At the same time, to attempt to continue to produce the Digest in Canada may well be an impossibility. Even should it prove possible, we would be forced to live eternally under the threat of further economic sanctions with the future of our business forever uncertain.

These words were written only a few hours after the statement of the Prime Minister and no details of his proposal had yet been placed before Parliament. At this moment, while we see clearly the outline of the cruel dilemma which we may soon face, we can only speculate on what our course of action would be if such a proposal became law. It will, in the final analysis, be up to Parliament to make a decision. In view of our record and of the welfare of the many Canadians whose livelihoods depend upon us, we would hope that an opportunity will be provided for us to state our case before Parliament in advance of any such decision.

But we can at this unhappy moment put to you, our readers, and to all fair-minded Canadians our humble conviction that it is totally unjust that the Digest in Canada be placed in such a situation. Surely the Digest's 19-year record in Canada should render it wholly immune, not merely half immune, from discriminatory legislation.

Is it too much to ask and hope that you, a Canadian reader of the Canadian Digest, interest yourself in this sore problem? May we suggest that, if you would like to know more about the problem, you write to me, the undersigned. As a Canadian, I am proud of our Canadian company. I would deem it a privilege to answer any questions you may have about its record and about this whole matter, and to provide you with any further explanations you might desire.

Yours truly,

E. P. Zimmerman, PRESIDENT
The Reader's Digest
Association (Canada) Ltd.

Source: Reader's Digest, March 1962.

AMENDMENTS TO THE INCOME TAX ACT

Limitations re advertising expense

12A. (1) In computing income, no deduction shall be made in respect of an otherwise deductible outlay or expense of a taxpayer for advertising space in an issue of a non-Canadian newspaper or periodical dated after December 31, 1965 for an advertisement directed primarily to a market in Canada.

(2) An issue or edition of an issue of any newspaper or periodical that is edited in whole or in part in Canada and printed and published in Canada and that was not on April 26, 1965 a Canadian newspaper or periodical shall be deemed, for the purposes of subsection (1), not to be an issue of a non-Canadian newspaper or periodical if

(a) throughout the period of 12 months ending April 26, 1965 issues or editions of issues of that publication were being edited in whole or in part in Canada and printed and published in Canada at the usual intervals for issues of that publication and have since that date continued to be so edited, printed and published without interruption except for a reason other than the cessation of the business of publishing that publication; and

(b) in the case of a periodical, the periodical is similar, in content and in respect of the class of readers to which it is directed, to the issues or editions of that periodical that were throughout the period of 12 months ending April 26, 1965 being edited in whole or in part in Canada and printed and published in Canada.

(3) Subsection (1) does not apply with respect to an advertisement in a special issue or edition of a newspaper that is edited in whole or in part and printed and published outside Canada if such special issue or edition is devoted

to features or news related primarily to Canada and the publishers thereof publish such an issue or edition not more frequently than twice a year.

(4) Subsection (1) does not apply with respect to an advertisement in

(a) a catalogue, or

(b) any publication the principal function of which is the encouragement, promotion or development of the fine arts, letters, scholarship or religion.

Definitions

(5) In this section,

Canadian Issue

(a) "Canadian issue" means,

(i) in relation to a newspaper, an issue, including a special issue,
  (A) the type of which, other than the type for advertisements or features, is set in Canada,
  (B) the whole of which, exclusive of any comics supplement, is printed in Canada,
  (C) that is edited in Canada by individuals resident in Canada, and
  (D) that is published in Canada, and
(ii) in relation to a periodical, an issue, including a special issue,
  (A) the type of which, other than the type for advertisements, is set in Canada,
  (B) that is printed in Canada,
  (C) that is edited in Canada by individuals resident in Canada, and
  (D) that is published in Canada,
      but does not include an issue of a periodical
  (E) that is produced or published under a licence granted by a person who produces or publishes issues of a periodical that are printed, edited or published outside Canada, or

(F) the contents of which, excluding advertisements, are substantially the same as the
contents of an issue of a periodical, or
the contents of one or more issues of one
or more periodicals, that was or were
printed, edited or published outside Canada;

Canadian Newspaper or Periodical

(b) "Canadian newspaper or periodical" means a newspaper or periodical the exclusive right to produce
and publish issues of which is held by one or more
of the following:

   (i) a Canadian citizen,
  (ii) a partnership of which at least 3/4 of the
       members are Canadian citizens and in which in-
       terests representing in value at least 3/4 of
       the total value of the partnership property
       are beneficially owned by Canadian citizens,
 (iii) an association or society of which at least
       3/4 of the members are Canadian citizens,
  (iv) Her Majesty in right of Canada or a province,
       or a municipality in Canada, or
   (v) a corporation
       (A) that is incorporated under the laws of
           Canada or a province,
       (B) of which the chairman or other presiding
           officer and at least 3/4 of the directors
           or other similar officers are Canadian
           citizens, and
       (C) of which, if it is a corporation having
           share capital, at least 3/4 of the shares
           having full voting rights under all circum-
           stances, and shares representing in the
           aggregate at least 3/4 of the paid-up
           capital, are beneficially owned by Cana-
           dian citizens or by corporations other than
           corporations controlled directly or indi-
           rectly by citizens or subjects of a country
           other than Canada; and

Issue of a Non-Canadian Newspaper or Periodical

    (c) "issue of a non-Canadian newspaper or periodical" means an issue that is not a Canadian issue of a Canadian newspaper or periodical.

Source: "The Income Tax Act," Revised Statutes of Canada 1952 (Ottawa: Queen's Printer, 1952), Chap. 148, as amended.

AMENDMENTS TO THE POST OFFICE ACT

Rates for
Canadian
newspapers
and
periodicals

(2) The rates of postage on Canadian newspapers and Canadian periodicals that may be transmitted by mail in Canada at the rates of postage specified in this section are as follows:

(a) on a daily Canadian newspaper,

(i) for the portion thereof not devoted to advertising, four cents a pound during the period commencing April 1, 1969 and ending September 30, 1969, four and one-half cents a pound during the period commencing October 1, 1969 and ending March 31, 1970, and five cents a pound thereafter, and

(ii) for the portion thereof devoted to advertising, nine cents a pound during the period commencing April 1, 1969 and ending September 30, 1969, twelve cents a pound during the period commencing October 1, 1969 and ending March 31, 1970, and fifteen cents a pound thereafter;

(b) on a weekly Canadian newspaper, four cents a pound during the period commencing April 1, 1969 and ending September 30, 1969, four and one-half cents a pound during the period commencing October 1, 1969 and ending March 31, 1970, and five cents a pound thereafter; and

(c) on all other Canadian newspapers and Canadian periodicals, four cents a pound during the period commencing April 1, 1969 and ending September 30, 1969, four and one-half cents a pound during the period commencing October 1, 1969 and ending March 31, 1970, and five cents a pound thereafter.

Minimum rate and free zone	(3) Notwithstanding subsection (2),
	(a) the minimum postage for a piece of mail consisting of one or more Canadian newspapers or Canadian periodicals described in paragraph (a), (b) or (c) of that subsection is two cents; and
	(b) where a weekly Canadian newspaper is published and mailed in Canada in a city, town or village having a population of not more than ten thousand persons, a total of twenty-five hundred copies of each issue of the newspaper may be transmitted by mail free of postage to post offices with no letter carrier services that are within a distance of forty miles from the known place of publication of the issue in such city, town or village.
Definitions	(4) In this section,
"Canadian newspaper" "Canadian periodical"	(a) "Canadian newspaper" or "Canadian periodical" means a regular or special issue of a newspaper or periodical, as the case may be,
	(i) the type of which, other than the type for advertisements, comic supplements or features, is set in Canada,
	(ii) the whole of which, other than advertisements, comic supplements or features, is printed in Canada,
	(iii) that is edited in Canada by individuals ordinarily resident in Canada, and
	(iv) that is published in Canada, but does not include an issue of a newspaper or periodical described in subparagraphs (i) to (iv) where
	(v) such issue is produced or published under a licence from a person who produces or publishes issues of a newspaper or periodical that are printed, edited or published outside Canada, or

(vi) the contents of such issue, excluding advertisements, comic supplements and features, are substantially the same as some or all of the contents of one or more issues of one or more newspapers or periodicals that are not first edited in Canada and are printed or published outside Canada;

"Daily Canadian newspaper"

(b) "daily Canadian newspaper" means a Canadian newspaper that is ordinarily published more frequently than once a week; and

"Weekly Canadian newspaper"

(c) "weekly Canadian newspaper" means a Canadian newspaper

(i) that is ordinarily published once a week,

(ii) that is intended primarily for the residents of a city, town or village and its surrounding community,

(iii) a substantial portion of each issue of which consists of news or other articles with respect to events and activities of interest primarily to the residents referred to in subparagraph (ii) for which it is primarily intended, and

(iv) the total circulation of which does not exceed ten thousand copies an issue.

Prescribed rates

12. A newspaper or periodical, other than a newspaper or periodical that may be transmitted by mail in Canada at the rates of postage specified in section 11, may be transmitted by mail at such postage rate as may be prescribed therefor by the regulations.

Source: Revised Statutes of Canada, 1968, 17 Elizabeth II, Chap. 5, pp. 30-33.

CANADIAN GOVERNMENT PERIODICALS

Name	Department	Annual Cost	Circulation
National Distribution			
Teamwork in Industry	Labour	30,000	46,500
Labour Gazette	Labour	210,000	16,500
Science Dimension	National Research Council	50,000	11,000
Canada's Mental Health	Health and Welfare	38,000	19,000
Health Education	Health and Welfare	12,000	3,000
Occupational Health Bulletin	Health and Welfare	4,000	13,500
Canada's Health and Welfare	Health and Welfare	38,000	50,000
Occupational Health Review	Health and Welfare	10,000	9,000
Nutrition Notes	Health and Welfare	7,000	7,000
Habitat	Central Mortgage and Housing Corp.	36,000	9,500
Low-Income Housing	Central Mortgage and Housing Corp.	24,000	4,800
Canadian Agriculture	Agriculture	12,000	3,500
Farm News	Agriculture	60,000	400,000
Lighter	Agriculture	4,000	1,700
Monthly Bulletin	External Affairs	35,000	4,500

Name	Department	Annual Cost	Circulation
National Distribution (continued)			
Flight Communication	Defence	20,000	2,300
Sentinel	Defence	170,000	47,000
Foreign Trade	Industry, Trade and Commerce	210,000	6,000
RCMP Quarterly	Royal Canadian Mounted Police	35,000	20,000
Fisheries of Canada	Fisheries	45,000	10,000
North	Indian Affairs and Northern Development	35,000	5,700
Indian News	Indian Affairs and Northern Development	75,000	55,000
Tawow	Indian Affairs and Northern Development	50,000	10,000
Inuttituut	Indian Affairs and Northern Development	8,000	2,500
North of 60	Indian Affairs and Northern Development	--	4,000
Optimum	Secretary of State	30,000	5,000
International Development	Canadian International Development Agency	30,000	29,000
International Distribution			
Canada Today	External Affairs	35,000	1,200
Weekly Bulletin	External Affairs	25,000	8,000

Name	Department	Annual Cost	Circulation
International Distribution (continued)			
Canadian Courier	Industry, Trade, and Commerce	150,000	190,000
Canadian Events	Canadian Government Travel Bureau	62,000	2,000,000
Internal Distribution			
Public Relations Notes	National Revenue	2,400	160
SI Bulletin	National Revenue	700	565
Management Memo	National Revenue	1,500	350
Communications 70	Post Office	50,000	50,000
Regular News	Post Office	8,000	12,000
Regular News	Post Office	8,000	12,000
Regular News	Post Office	8,000	13,000
Regular News	Post Office	8,000	13,000
Magazine	Post Office	40,000	50,000
Dispatch	Public Works	15,000	8,000
News	Public Works	2,000	8,000
Impressions	Queen's Printer	8,000	1,500
The Link	Fisheries	4,000	2,000
Perspective	Central Mortgage and Housing Corporation	23,000	1,800
Dialogue	Labour	6,000	850
Shape	Consumer Affairs	4,000	2,000
Carillon	Veterans Affairs	20,000	12,000

Name	Department	Annual Cost	Circulation
Internal Distribution (continued)			
Transport Canada	Transport	20,000	12,500
Profile	Regional Economic Expansion	8,000	2,500
Participation	Secretary of State	12,000	1,500
Perspective	Health and Welfare	16,000	8,000
Intercom	Indian Affairs and Northern Development	25,000	7,000
Manpower and Immigration Digest	Manpower and Immigration	16,000	10,000
Atlantic Breeze	Manpower and Immigration	6,000	1,000
Journal of Manpower and Immigration	Manpower and Immigration	3,000	2,500
Roundtable	Manpower and Immigration	2,500	2,700
Prairie Points	Manpower and Immigration	600	1,100
News-Views	Manpower and Immigration	2,000	1,100
Entre-Nous	Treasury Board	8,000	1,500

Source: "Report on Government Non-Technical Periodical Publishing," memo, Information Canada, Ottawa, 1971.

ISAIAH ALLAN LITVAK is Professor of Economics and International Affairs at Carleton University.

Dr. Litvak was born in Shanghai, China, where he received his early education. He left Shanghai in 1948 for Montreal, Canada, where he received his Bachelor of Commerce degree at McGill University. He took his Master of Science and Doctorate degrees at Columbia University; prior to joining Carleton in 1970, he taught for nine years at McMaster University, first in the Department of Political Economy and later in the Graduate School of Business. Dr. Litvak has lectured extensively at various universities and institutes in North America, Europe, and Africa. He is an executive member of various learned societies and serves on the editorial boards of a number of journals.

Professor Litvak's recent research has dealt with multinational enterprise and government-business relations.

Dr. Litvak has acquired considerable practical, as well as academic, experience: since 1960 he has served as a management consultant to Canadian federal and provincial governments in the area of industrial policy and has been a consultant to business in North America and Europe.

In his field of specialization his publications include: Dual Loyalty: Canadian-U.S. Business Arrangements, coauthored with C. J. Maule and R. D. Robinson (New York: McGraw-Hill, 1971); Foreign Investment: The Experience of Host Countries, coedited with C. J. Maule (New York: Praeger Publishers, 1970); Marketing: Canada, coedited with B. E. Mallen (New York: McGraw-Hill, 1968); Canadian Cases in Marketing, coauthored with P. M. Banting (New York: McGraw-Hill, 1968); The Nation Keepers (New York: McGraw-Hill, 1967); and Trading with the Communists (Behind the Headlines Series, Canadian Institute of International Affairs (Toronto, 1963). His articles have appeared in various journals including The Journal of World Trade Law, Industrial Relations, Columbia Journal of World Business, Journal of Conflict Resolution, California Management Review, Science Forum, The Business Quarterly, and The Canadian Journal of Public Administration.

CHRISTOPHER JOHN MAULE is Associate Professor of Economics and International Affairs at Carleton University.

He was educated at the University of British Columbia and Queen's University and received his doctorate at the London School of Economics. Prior to joining the Carleton University, Dr. Maule taught at McMaster University.

In recent years, Dr. Maule's research has dealt with topics in industrial organization and international investment. He has also acted as a consultant to industry and government. Publications include Dual Loyalty: Canadian-U.S. Business Arrangements, coauthored with I. A. Litvak and R. D. Robinson (New York: McGraw-Hill, 1971) and Foreign Investment: The Experience of Host Countries, coedited with I. A. Litvak (New York: Praeger Publishers, 1970). Articles have appeared in various journals including the Journal of Law and Economics, the Journal of Industrial Economics, the Journal of World Trade Law, the Journal of Conflict Resolution, Industrial Relations, Pacific Affairs, Columbia Journal of World Business, the Business Quarterly, and the Canadian Journal of Public Administration.

ASPEN NOTEBOOK ON GOVERNMENT AND THE MEDIA
     edited by William L. Rivers and
     Michael J. Nyhan

CHILDREN'S TELEVISION COMMERCIALS: A Content Analysis
     Charles Winick, Lorne G. Williamson,
     Stuart F. Chuzmir, and
     Mariann Pezzella Winick

FOREIGN INVESTMENT: The Experience of Host Countries (1970)
     edited by Isaiah A. Litvak and
     Christopher J. Maule

THE IMPACT OF U.S. INVESTMENT IN EUROPE: A Case Study of
the Automotive and Computer Industries
     Y. S. Hu

MANAGING FOREIGN INVESTMENT IN SOUTHERN ITALY: U.S.
Business in Developing Areas of the EEC
     Douglas F. Lamont

THE MULTINATIONAL ENTERPRISE AND THE THIRD WORLD: The
Nationalization of Alcan-Dembe
     Isaiah A. Litvak and Christopher J. Maule